KID

CONFIDENT

#3

How to Handle
STRESS
for Middle School Success

KID CONFIDENT

#3

How to Handle
STRESS
for Middle School Success

by Silvi Guerra, PsyD   illustrated by DeAndra Hodge

Imagination Press · Washington, DC · American Psychological Association

For all middle schoolers who are brave enough to ask for help, are willing to learn new things, and hold hope that things will get better with effort. You are my heroes.

For the families and clients who have trusted me to support their growth throughout the years. I'm profoundly grateful to be part of your journey.

For Rümi, my unconditional comfort, support, and loyal friend. Thank you for choosing me.

Te quiero tanto mi chiquita.—SG

To Anna, Rebekah, and Lincoln, my best friends since middle school. Thank you for making me who I am today—DH

Books for Kids From the
American Psychological Association

Copyright © 2023 by Silvi Guerra. Illustrations copyright © 2023 by DeAndra Hodge. Published in 2023 by Magination Press, an imprint of the American Psychological Association. All rights reserved. Except as permitted under the United States Copyright Act of 1976, no part of this publication may be reproduced or distributed in any form or by any means, or stored in a database or retrieval system, without the prior written permission of the publisher.

Magination Press is a registered trademark of the American Psychological Association. Order books at maginationpress.org or call 1-800-374-2721.

Series editor: Bonnie Zucker, PsyD

Book design by Rachel Ross

Printed by Lake Book Manufacturing, Inc., Melrose Park, IL

Library of Congress Cataloging-in-Publication Data
Names: Guerra, Silvi, author. | Hodge, DeAndra, illustrator.
Title: How to handle STRESS for middle school success: kid confident book 3/Silvi Guerra, DeAndra Hodge.
Description: Washington, DC: Magination Press, 2023. | Series: Kid confident: Middle grade shelf help | Includes bibliographical references. | Summary: "Middle grade kids learn about stress and anxiety, how it manifests physiologically and cognitively, and how to keep balance and cope with stress"—Provided by publisher.
Identifiers: LCCN 2022031892 (print) | LCCN 2022031893 (ebook) | ISBN 9781433838163 (hardcover) | ISBN 9781433838170 (ebook)
Subjects: LCSH: Stress in children—Juvenile literature. | Anxiety in children—Juvenile literature. | Stress management for children—Juvenile literature. | BISAC: JUVENILE NONFICTION/ Social Topics / Emotions & Feelings | JUVENILE NONFICTION/Health & Daily Living/General
Classification: LCC BF723.S75 G84 2023 (print) | LCC BF723.S75 (ebook) | DDC 155.4/189042—dc23/eng/20220811
LC record available at https://lccn.loc.gov/2022031892
LC ebook record available at https://lccn.loc.gov/2022031893

Manufactured in the United States of America

10 9 8 7 6 5 4 3 2

CONTENTS

DEAR READER (DON'T SKIP THIS!)

You may have picked up this book because you're feeling stressed about middle school, or maybe someone who cares about you gave you this book. Regardless of how you got here, I'm happy you've decided to learn more about yourself and ways to handle stress and the dreaded worry brain.

 What is "worry brain," you ask?

Well, **worry brain** is when you're going about your day, attending your classes, sports, or hanging out with your friends and, suddenly, your heart may start beating fast, or your cheeks feel hot and then worry thoughts flood your brain, which may sound like:

 Have you ever had thoughts like these?

Middle school can be stressful. You may have rocked elementary school and now you're entering this new chapter in your life as a student. You might be feeling like the workload has increased and that your teachers are counting on you to be more independent. This book is here to help guide you through the process of understanding what worries are and how they show up, and sometimes mess stuff up. It will also teach you helpful strategies to manage your stress better, so it doesn't get in the way of the things that matter the most to you, like accomplishing your goals and feeling good about yourself and your life.

When I was in middle school, I would have loved a book like this because I struggled with worries myself. I put a lot of thought into making this book as helpful and fun as possible for you! This book is like a video game, and each chapter that you complete, you'll have the opportunity to **LEVEL UP YOUR STRESS MANAGEMENT SKILLS.**

You will learn key skills that will help you understand yourself better and help you be the **BOSS OF YOUR BRAIN.** These important life skills will not only support you navigating middle school better but will also benefit you in the long run as you become an older teen and, eventually, an adult.

THE LEVEL UP SKILLS INCLUDE:

- Understanding **how stress shows up,**
- Knowing how to keep your **health in check** to manage your worries,
- Using **Chill-Out Hacks** to help you calm down when you need to the most,
- Developing a **formula for bravery** to help you feel courageous throughout middle school,
- Having an **"I GOT THIS!"** attitude to work towards your goals and not give up, and
- Having **more control** over the way you respond to stress.

You can read this book cover to cover or choose the chapters that you need the most. I recommend you have a notebook or piece of paper with you to answer questions and complete helpful quests along that way. Remember you're not doing this alone. You have this book and me as your dedicated worry coach!

–Coach Silvi

NOW, ARE YOU READY TO

LEVEL

UP?

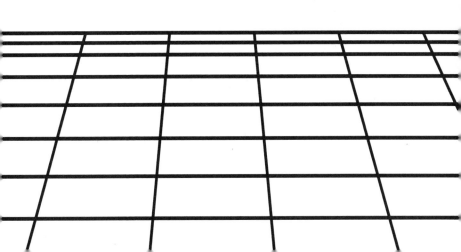

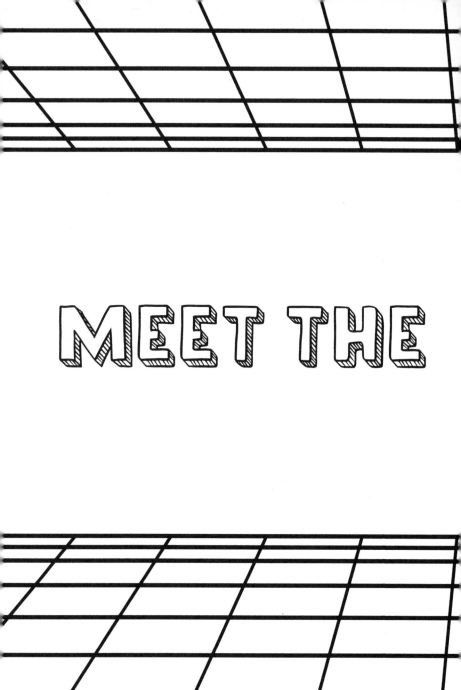

MEET THE

MEET PLAYER 1: OTTO

Otto is a kind and funny guy. He's into surfing, skateboarding, and playing video games with his friends. He does well in school, but when it comes time to speak up or present in front of the class, he freezes, feels his heart beating very fast, and often forgets what he practiced the night before. He procrastinates on group projects because he doesn't look forward to having to speak in front of his classmates and often avoids raising his hand in class even when he's confident he has the right answer. Sometimes, on days when he knows he has to talk in front of his class, he will toss and turn the whole night before, have trouble getting out of bed in the morning, and won't be able to eat his usual breakfast because he has a stomachache.

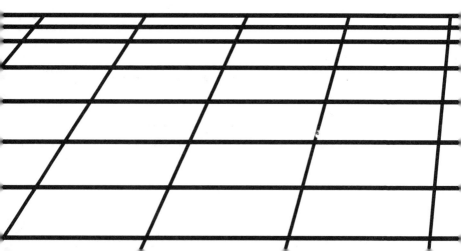

MEET PLAYER 2: LUNA

Luna is a sweet and confident girl. She enjoys rock climbing and playing on her school's field hockey team. Luna has straight As in all her classes and stresses out over her grades all the time. Most nights of the week you'll find Luna going to bed late working on assignments because she never seems to have enough time to finish before her 9PM bedtime. Luna wants her assignments to be "perfect" for her teachers, and sometimes will re-write her notes and assignments to get it "just right." Luna often worries for days ahead of time when she has a test coming up, thinking she won't have time to prepare. Luna has been getting headaches and is having trouble sleeping because school stress is taking over.

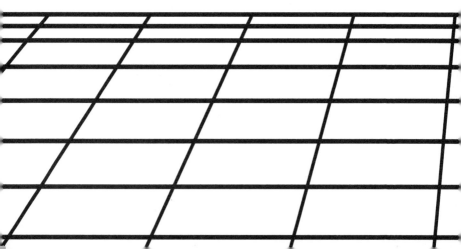

Luna

MOTTO

Take the first step, then another!

LEVEL UP STRENGTHS

Ambitious • Responsible • Disciplined •
Organized • Positive attitude

STRESSORS

Tending to be self-critical • Wanting things
to be perfect • Overthinking

STRESS LEVEL INDICATOR

8

0   1   2   3   4   5   6   7   8   9   10

MEET PLAYER 3: ROWAN

Rowan is creative and fun to be around. Rowan identifies as non-binary and their preferred pronouns are they/them. They grew up in a big family and can always be counted on to come up with games to play and adventures to go on. Rowan loves participating in stage crew for the school's theatre program and is also Head Editor of the school blog and social media accounts. They enjoy graphic design and photography as well, which makes their posts really fun to follow on Instagram and TikTok. Rowan has big goals they'd like to accomplish, like running for student government and auditioning for the school play. But Rowan gets impatient while working towards their goals. They feel like if they don't get what they want right away, or don't get something right the first time, they want to quit altogether. Accomplishing goals that take time, like preparing and auditioning for the school play or coming up with a campaign to run for student government, is hard for Rowan because they tend to procrastinate. They avoid doing the work by posting or scrolling through social media and hanging out with friends instead.

Rowan

MOTTO

Teamwork makes the dream work!

LEVEL UP STRENGTHS

Creative • Leader • Curious and loves to learn •
Team player • Open minded

STRESSORS

Procrastinating • Fearing rejection • Being impulsive •
Quitting when things are hard • Easily discouraged

STRESS LEVEL INDICATOR

5.5

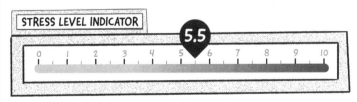

A NOTE FOR THE ADULTS IN YOUR LIFE

Hola and Hello!

I'm so grateful that you've joined your middle schooler on this journey to overcome stress and worries. The middle school years can be challenging as students are expected to be more independent academically while also navigating social stress and peer groups changing. These changes will test their resilience and present a variety of stressors that bring about both challenges and growth. Research shows that transitioning from elementary to middle school, while exciting, is also a time of tension associated with an increase in anxiety. This is why I believe that the building of middle schoolers' mental, emotional, and physical resources to manage stressors will serve to bolster their independence and resilience, as well as provide a protective factor throughout their development.

I know from personal experience that anxiety can be an invisible struggle. On the outside, children can look like they are thriving. On the inside, they may have a hard time making decisions, staying on top of their work, and keeping friends. That means it's often overlooked. That's why I've dedicated my life and career to helping children, teens, and adults who experience anxiety understand themselves better with a bountiful toolbox of strategies to manage stress.

This book will prepare your middle schooler to "level up!" by teaching them a variety of evidence-based skills to foster healthier and more effective coping. Cognitive-behavioral therapy (CBT), an effective and proven treatment approach, will be utilized to offer strategies and solutions such as how to recognize and question common thinking errors and learn coping skills that support self-soothing and emotional regulation. Additionally, the relationship between mind and body will be discussed and your child will learn how to maintain a healthy balance through proper diet, exercise, sleep hygiene, and mindfulness practice (to support focus, grounding, and relaxation).

This book will emphasize developing an internal locus of control and an "I got this!" attitude based on Carol Dweck and Angela Duckworth's work on growth mindset and grit. Your child will learn about having an optimistic mindset and how to cope with stress in positive ways. Research shows that happiness, which is a combination of being satisfied with one's life, having access to coping resources, and the experience of positive emotions, predicts positive life outcomes. The skills taught in this book will contribute greatly to your child's resilience in life.

I invite you to go through this book with your child, cheer on their efforts to try new strategies, and encourage them by letting them know that they are becoming the "expert on stress management" at home. Cheering your child on gives them a strong sense of mastery and confidence that they can learn important skills... and can be a resource to the entire family!

I'm excited to go on this journey with you and your middle schooler!

With gratitude,
Silvi Guerra, PsyD

LEVEL

1

STRESS
EXPLAINED

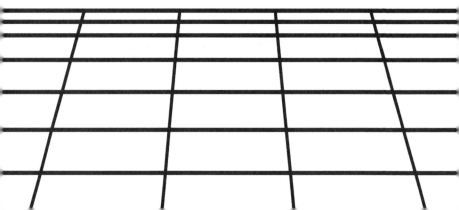

ur three players all struggle with stress and worries in different ways. Otto's worries have to do with performing in front of other people. He stresses out over being judged by others. These worries make completing assignments hard and can sometimes ruin his whole day! Luna is so worried she'll make a mistake that she gets stuck and spends way too much time on her schoolwork. Luna wants to be A+ student, but the stress and worries that keep her stuck working long hours most school nights impact her mood and her relationships with her family and friends. Then there's Rowan, who has big goals they want to accomplish, but their fear of rejection or messing up along the way keeps them from trying new things and working towards these dreams. All of our players' stress and worries get in the way of their schoolwork, their relationships, and their goals.

 Do you see yourself in any of the players? Where would you rate your stress level today?

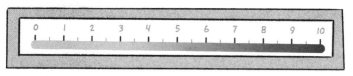

Seems to me like they're all ready to level up their stress management skills to make their middle school years more successful! Join them on their journey to see how we can help each of them (and YOU!) figure out how to not let stress get in the way of schoolwork, friendships, and overall happiness.

LET'S START WITH LEARNING THE BASICS ABOUT STRESS. You've probably heard people say, "I'm so stressed out!" or "This is so stressful." You may have mostly heard adults saying things like this before, but the fact is that kids have lots of things going on in their lives that can cause stress too.

Have you ever had days when you had so much homework that you had trouble sleeping? Have you ever felt sick to your stomach during a test? Have you ever felt so worried about something that you got a headache? If you have, then you know what it's like to feel stressed.

 **What is this stress thing anyway?**

STRESS IS WHAT YOU FEEL WHEN YOU ARE WORRIED OR UNCOMFORTABLE ABOUT SOMETHING. Stress also shows up when you feel scared about what might happen in the future. You might not know this, but your brain was built for this! There is a very good reason your body is responding this way when you feel stressed. Stress is your body's natural response to keep you safe.

Stress can show up in different ways. It can make you think things like, "I'll never be able to pass that test!" or "There's no way I'll have time to complete all my homework." It can also show up in the way your body feels, like your heart starts beating fast or you start sweating when speaking in front of a group of people. It can also present itself in your behaviors when you avoid answering your friend's FaceTime calls, or ask your parents over and over whether it's safe to take off your mask to eat at school.

 **Can you relate? What are some ways that stress shows up for you?**

THERE IS GOOD STRESS (ALSO CALLED EUSTRESS) AND BAD STRESS (ALSO KNOWN AS DISTRESS). REALLY!

Good Stress motivates you to work towards your goals and dreams. When you face a problem or situation that you think you can handle, you experience good stress. For example, when Otto was first learning to surf, he felt good stress every time he was able to stand on the board and catch a wave. **Bad Stress,** on the other hand, happens when you feel you're in a threatening situation and you don't feel like you'll be able to survive it! Bad stress makes you feel bad, scared, and stuck when trying to accomplish your goals.

GOOD STRESS

- Motivates you
- Makes you focus on your goals
- Feels exciting sometimes!
- Helps you get better at new things like surfing, field hockey, and learning your Spanish vocabulary words

EXAMPLES:

- Being asked to accept an award at school for doing a great job on a project
- Trying out for a new sport you've really been wanting to play
- Nailing the theater audition you've been practicing so hard for
- Asking someone for their phone number or their social media handle

BAD STRESS

- Causes upset or concern
- Makes you feel out of control in your body
- Decreases your ability to work toward your goals

EXAMPLES:

- The death of a family pet
- Injury or illness for yourself or someone you love
- Sleep problems
- Fighting with your family or friends
- Being bullied

Good and bad stress happen to **ALL OF US!** The goal is to level up your stress management skills so that you are in charge of how you feel rather than letting worries call the shots.

 But when is stress a problem?

STRESS IS A PROBLEM WHEN IT HAPPENS ALL THE TIME OR INTERFERES WITH YOUR ABILITY TO COMPLETE YOUR RESPONSIBILITIES, such as:

- Being a kind family member, friend, teammate, or classmate
- Focusing in class
- Completing homework
- Getting enough sleep

Remember that a little stress (or **Good Stress**) can be helpful. A lot of stress can be harmful because it takes away your ability to be the awesome person you are.

WHEN STRESS IS MESSING STUFF UP, IT'S TIME TO LEVEL UP!

Let's see how our players do in stressful situations. Think you can catch good and bad stress moments now? Let's see those Level Up skills in action.

QUEST
GOOD & BAD STRESS

Rowan wants to be a part of student government this year. They see that the deadline to sign up is tomorrow. They ask their friend Amy, who also wants to be part of student government, to stay after school today to complete the application together so they don't miss the deadline.

 Good stress or bad stress moment?

If you thought Rowan rocked this stressful situation, you're right! Rowan asked their friend Amy for support, so they wouldn't miss the deadline.

Otto falls off his board at the skate park in front of his friends. He notices them laugh at him and he tries the trick again and falls again. He gets home and his mom asks how his day went. He picks a fight with her, slams his bedroom door, and refuses to come down for dinner.

 **Good or bad stress moment?**

Otto experienced some bad stress when he felt embarrassed that he didn't land the ollie like he wanted and then took it out on his mom when he got home. His worries got the best of him.

WHEN WORRY IS AT THE WHEEL

SIGNS OF STRESS

Everyone experiences stress, and it can show up in different ways. So, what does stress look like? How does it show up in your body, and what are the signs that **Worry Brain** is calling the shots?

STRESS SIGNS

- ☐ Having trouble sleeping
- ☐ Having racing or repetitive thoughts that won't go away
- ☐ Trying to control people or events by over-planning
- ☐ Not following directions from parents or teachers
- ☐ Avoiding activities or events
- ☐ Having stomachaches or headaches
- ☐ Crying or having difficulty managing big emotions like sadness, disappointment, and anger

 Do any of these sound like you?

Let's take a look at how stress shows up in each of our players:

Rowan signed up for student government and now needs to pick a slogan for their campaign. Since signing up to participate in the election, they've been really busy and aren't eating lunch with their friends very often anymore. Sometimes their friends or parents have to remind them to eat.

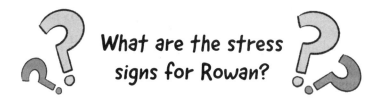

What are the stress signs for Rowan?

If you noticed "loss of appetite," you are correct. Nice job!

Otto was worried about soccer tryouts today. He asked his mom to remind him to pack his cleats, but just before tryouts he realized that they were not in his gym bag. His friend Maya came up to him to wish him luck and he snapped at her and said "I won't make the team anyway!" and walked away from Maya in a huff.

What are the stress signs for Otto?

If you said "forgetting things" and "irritability," or "mean behaviors towards his friend Maya," you got it! Luckily, Otto's dad dropped off his cleats before school ended, he was able to try out, and made the team.

Luna has a field hockey tournament this weekend. She also told her friend Alana that she'd go to her birthday party on Friday night. She was trying to plan out her week so she can get everything done that she needed to. She made five separate to-do lists and scheduled her days down to the half-hour to make sure she didn't miss anything before Friday comes.

What are the stress signs for Luna?

If you noticed Luna "over-planning" her week with lists and high expectations for herself, you're spot on!

IT'S YOUR TURN: TIME TO COMPLETE YOUR LEVEL I QUEST! Think of ways stress shows up for you. Are you an over-planner like Luna? Do you get headaches when you feel overwhelmed? Maybe you are quick to anger like Otto when feeling stressed? Make a mental list or write down three ways that stress shows up for you. These are your **Stress Signs**—recognizing them will help you level up and be ready to become a stress management expert.

LEVEL UP

SKILLS LEARNED

 Stress is normal. It happens to all of us! There is good stress and bad stress.

 When you face a problem or situation that you can handle, that motivates or even excites you, you experience **Good Stress.**

 When you are in a threatening or uncomfortable situation or you don't feel like you can handle it, you experience **Bad Stress.**

 Knowing your **Stress Signs** helps you know when you need help. When stress and worries are excessive, you'll need strategies and support to feel better.

CONGRATULATIONS ON COMPLETING LEVEL 1! YOU'RE ON YOUR WAY TO BECOMING A STRESS EXPERT!

YOUR BRAIN &
THE THREE PARTS
OF STRESS

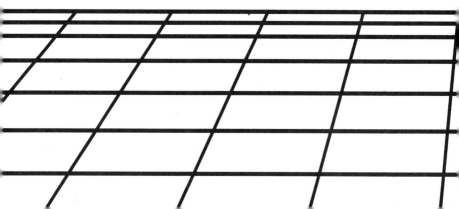

id you know that your brain is like a supercomputer? Your brain is in charge of **EVERYTHING** that you do! Your brain is a powerful organ that gives you the tools to learn new things, adapt, and be successful. Your brain has a pretty important job! Don't you think?

YOUR BRAIN HELPS YOU:

- Think and remember things
- Communicate with others
- Move your body
- Experience emotions, big and small

The brain has different parts that each have an important job. Let's do some exploring inside your amazing brain!

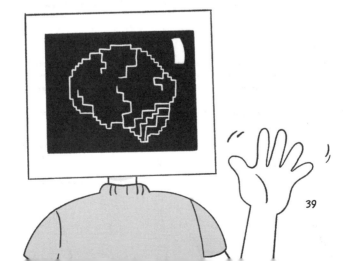

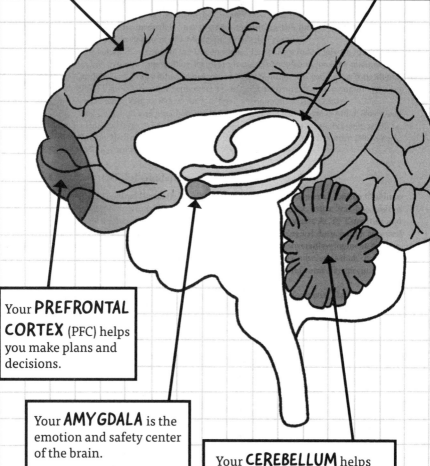

Your **CEREBRUM** helps you think and speak. It also controls your ability to read and learn new things. It also controls your five senses, which include your ability to see, hear, smell, touch, and taste.

Your **HIPPOCAMPUS** is where memories are formed. Think of it like a computer folder where you can store and access your memories when needed.

Your **PREFRONTAL CORTEX** (PFC) helps you make plans and decisions.

Your **AMYGDALA** is the emotion and safety center of the brain.

Your **CEREBELLUM** helps with your ability to balance (like on a surfboard or skateboard) and develop your motor skills. This means that it assists your muscles in coordinating movement, allowing you to walk, play sports, dance, and ride a bike.

As you can see, every part of your supercomputer has an important job. The two parts of the brain that mostly relate to your stress are:

THE PREFRONTAL CORTEX (PFC). Your PFC is often called the executive center or boss of the brain because it helps you make plans and decisions. The PFC also helps you accomplish your goals by helping you figure out what steps you need to take to make them happen. It also helps you with self-control and thinking things through to consider the consequences of your actions.

THE AMYGDALA. This is the part of your brain that controls your emotions, and one of its most important jobs is to keep you safe. I call it the "safety center" of the brain because it's always scanning your environment for potential threats and danger. This part of the brain is going to be really important as you level up your stress management skills. When your amygdala perceives any sort of threat, anything from seeing a bee, to not getting a text back from your friend, or feeling nervous about an upcoming project, your brain has four responses to keep you safe: fight, flight, freeze, or fawn. More on that next!

QUEST

PARTS OF THE BRAIN AND THEIR JOBS

For this Level 2 Quest, grab a piece of paper and try to match the part of the brain to its important job. You got this!

QUEST: Parts of the Brain and Their Jobs

_____1. Cerebrum

a. This part of your brain is behind your forehead and helps you make plans and decisions.

_____2. Cerebellum

b. This is a tightly packed group of cells deep inside the center of your brain. This area controls your emotions.

_____3. Prefrontal Cortex (PFC)

c. This is the largest part of your brain. It helps you think and speak. It's also in charge or your five senses.

_____4. Hippocampus

d. This is the center part of your brain where you store memories and information.

_____5. Amygdala

e. This is a small area in the back of your brain that helps you coordinate your movements and muscles.

KEY: 1. c, 2. e, 3. a, 4. d, 5. b

STRESS RESPONSES

Picture it: a long, long time ago, cavemen and women lived among wild animals. A caveman wasn't larger, stronger, or faster than a lion, for example. Instead, ancient humans had to develop quick responses to dangerous situations to outsmart potential predators and keep themselves safe.

WHEN YOU ARE PRESENTED WITH A SCARY, STRESSFUL, OR DANGEROUS SITUATION, YOUR BRAIN WILL AUTOMATICALLY RESPOND TO KEEP YOU SAFE.

The amygdala generates these responses. The amygdala is your safety center, remember? These responses are physical reactions that happen when you are stressed or scared, and they are completely out of your control. They happen automatically! It is your body's natural reaction to perceived danger. Each response instantly causes hormonal and physical changes in your body. These changes allow you to act quickly so you can protect yourself. It's a survival instinct that your ancestors developed many years ago.

There are four different types of safety reactions, and they are called **Fight, Flight, Freeze**, or **Fawn** responses. A **Fight** response supports your ability to protect yourself by getting ready to attack in response to a perceived threat. For cavemen and cavewomen this meant getting a spear and doing their best to fight with the wild animal until it was no longer a threat. In modern times, this may look like fighting with your parents when you're stressed about schoolwork or arguing with a friend who let you down.

THIS IS THE LAST TIME YOU INTERRUPT OUR DINNER TO STEAL OUR FOOD!

A **Flight** response helps you run away from stressful situations. This might look like actually running away, but may also show up as avoiding stressful situations altogether, like not wanting to go to a party where you don't know many people or refusing to ride a rollercoaster that you've never been on before.

The **Freeze** response is when you stay completely still (frozen) in order to get ready for the next move to keep yourself safe. Fun fact about this stress response: freezing is an evolutionary survival tactic, similar to when an animal plays dead. Animals instinctively know not to attack another animal if it looks like it's already dead. Why? Because the dead animal might have been sick or may already be decomposing, and could make the attacker sick (unless the "attacking" animal is a scavenger who has evolved to be able to eat dead things!). The Freeze response might look like staying completely still and remaining quiet while your teacher corrects your behavior, or like standing in front of class before a presentation and not being able to move or remember what to say because you're worried you'll mess up or you feel embarrassed speaking in front of others.

Then there's the **Fawn** response. This is your brain's attempt to avoid conflict or confrontation by pleasing others. Fawning means that you attend to the needs of others in a way that ignores your own emotions and needs. For example, you might have just been assigned a math teacher that you've heard is really tough on students. Your Fawn response might be to be a "good kid" and student in their class and participate as much as possible (even when you don't feel like it), or to avoid asking them questions about a lesson you don't understand because you're afraid it'll upset them.

Time for another Quest!

QUEST

IDENTIFY THE STRESS RESPONSE

For this Level 2 Quest, identify the stress response the players are experiencing. Grab a piece of paper or write on your notebook whether they are responding in fight, flight, freeze, or fawn mode.

Tip: some scenarios can have two stress responses.

Luna's field hockey practice ran late and now she's going to be late to her friend's birthday party. Luna tells her mom she prefers not to go because she'll feel embarrassed to walk in after all her friends are already there.

 Which response is this? Fight, Flight, Freeze or Fawn?

Rowan's student council advisor is known for being strict and expecting the student council members to arrive on time and be completely prepared for meetings. Rowan finds themselves getting to meetings 15 minutes early and always brings cookies for the group to share.

Which response is this? Fight, Flight, Freeze or Fawn?

Otto was playing basketball with friends and a player on the other team was playing defense pretty aggressively. At one point in the game, he thought that player even tried to trip him. When the game ended, instead of shaking that player's hand, he pushed him and said, "Don't ever do that to me again!" and walked away upset.

Which response is this? Fight, Flight, Freeze or Fawn?

If you guessed that Luna engaged in Flight response because she wanted to avoid her friend's birthday party, you are right! She didn't want to feel embarrassed and chose to not attend altogether. She did feel serious FOMO when she saw the videos her friends posted on TikTok after the party though.

Rowan was showing the Fawn response by arriving to meetings extra early and also bringing snacks for everyone because they were intimidated by their student council advisor and wanted to please them.

Then there's Otto, who was definitely showing us his Fight as well as his Flight response. He shoved the player that was playing aggressively because he felt threatened by him, and then also walked away to avoid any additional interactions.

SYSTEM UPDATES

Now that you know all about your supercomputer and how it helps keep you safe, it's important to understand that just like a computer or tech device, your brain needs regular updates. Your brain has the ability to learn, change, and adapt, and this is called **neuroplasticity**. When you learn something new or have a new experience, you create new connections in your brain, and this updates your supercomputer to be ready to adapt to new circumstances. This happens on a daily basis, but it's also something that you can support with your actions and your thoughts. This is the first step in becoming the boss of your brain and worries!

For example, do you remember the first time you took a swim or dance lesson, or even learned to use an electric scooter? That first time you were probably thinking, "There's NO WAY I'm going to be able to do that! This seems too scary and too hard." But because these were things you wanted to learn, you showed up to swim or dance class, or maybe you asked an adult to help you learn how ride a scooter, and after that first time, you may have thought, "That was easier than I thought." Then the next time it was a little easier too. With practice, now you can swim like a fish, dance choreographed dances, or ride that scooter like a pro, and no longer feel scared or hesitant! That's neuroplasticity.

THINK + FEEL + DO

YOUR THOUGHTS ARE SO POWERFUL! The words in your mind can make you feel good or bad and can cause you to make helpful or unhelpful choices. This is how it works—something happens and then you have a thought about it (you **THINK**), then you have a feeling or body sensation about it (you **FEEL**), and then you might engage in a behavior because of how you feel (you **DO)**.

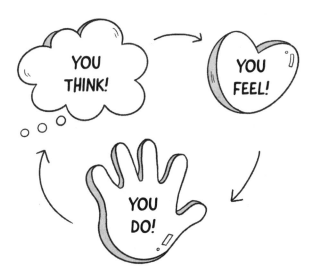

Following this cycle, you can break down a Stress Response into three parts: (1) What you think, (2) What you feel, and (3) What you do when you're stressed, anxious, or upset.

Scientists have developed a bunch of strategies based on this **Think + Feel + Do** thing and what we know about neuroplasticity. These are called cognitive-behavioral therapy (CBT) approaches. CBT skills have been studied for many years and are proven to be super helpful in overcoming worries and leveling up your stress management skills. These CBT strategies focus on how your thoughts affect your emotions and behavior. And since your brain has the ability to learn, change, and adapt, you may be wondering, *If I change how I think about something, can I change how I feel and what I do?*

Short answer: **YES!**

THE POWER IS IN YOUR THOUGHTS. Updating your brain and stress management skills starts with your thoughts. (We will get to the other parts of the stress cycle in later chapters. Remember that what you think, you feel, then you do!) Check out how Luna and Rowan experienced the same situation but responded to it in totally different ways...

HERE'S THE SITUATION: Luna and Rowan have not received an invitation to their mutual friend, Alana's, birthday party.

She thinks: I know Alana is my friend and maybe she just didn't have my email address.
She feels: OK and curious about when she'll receive her invitation.
She does: Continues focusing on her schoolwork for the day and preparing for her field hockey game later.

They think: That's so rude! Alana and I are supposed to be friends. Why wouldn't she invite me to her birthday party?!
They feel: Upset and confused.
They do: Avoids Alana at school because they're assuming she's mad at them, and sulks during lunch with their friends because they're bummed about the situation.

Outcome: Alana asked Luna and Rowan for their email addresses the next day since she didn't have them, and they both got their invites that night.

Did you notice Rowan having a harder time than Luna? Rowan had a **Hot Thought** about the situation (*That's so rude! Alana and I are supposed to be friends. Why wouldn't she invite me to her birthday party?!*) while Luna remained curious about what may have happened (*I know Alana is my friend and she must not have my email address*). A **Hot Thought** is an instant negative reaction to a perceived threat or problem. We all have them sometimes, just like Rowan did. But, you can change your thoughts, to change the way you feel and what you do, right? Let's do a mini quest to try this out.

You may be asking, "how do I change my Hot Thought?" I got you! Let's learn two Mental Hacks (a.k.a. **CBT stress management strategies**) that will help you change those hot thoughts to helpful thoughts instead.

QUEST
THE POWER OF YET

Next time you have a Hot Thought, try adding the word "**Yet**" to that thought. Check out how it works.

EMBRACE THE POWER OF... YET!

Like you've been learning, the thoughts and words you use really play a role in how you feel and what you do. That's when the power of YET can really help you out. Using the word "yet" when you're having a Hot Thought helps you realize that any goal takes work and effort over time. Sometimes your Hot Thoughts keep you stuck in your ways. Adding the word "yet" allows you to feel more hopeful and to focus on finding a solution, rather than just focusing on the problem.

ANOTHER USEFUL MENTAL HACK IS CALLED A THOUGHT RECORD. Thought records are a tool to help you recognize and change hot or unhelpful thoughts to helpful ones. The purpose of the **Thought Record** is to help you learn and create the habit of paying attention to your thoughts and working to change them to be more balanced and based on facts (not fears). Remember, if you change your thoughts, you change the way you feel, and what you do! Here's an example:

THOUGHT RECORD					
STRESSFUL SITUATION	HOT THOUGHT	HOW DID YOU FEEL RIGHT AWAY?	IS THERE ANOTHER WAY TO LOOK AT THE SITUATION?	COUNTER-THOUGHT	HOW DO YOU FEEL NOW?
I got a C on my math test.	I'm not good at math! I'm going to fail the class.	Crummy, not smart.	I didn't do well on this test but on the last two tests I got an A and a B.	I didn't do well on this test, but I can prepare more for the next one and bring up my grade.	Better! In control.

  Wondering what parts of your brain you are using for this mental hack? The amygdala and the PFC!

QUEST

THOUGHT RECORD

For this final Level 2 Quest, grab a piece of paper and create a Thought Record using the table here as a guide.

THOUGHT RECORD

STRESSFUL SITUATION	HOT THOUGHT	HOW DID YOU FEEL RIGHT AWAY?	IS THERE ANOTHER WAY TO LOOK AT THE SITUATION?	COUNTER-THOUGHT	HOW DO YOU FEEL NOW?
Describe what happened.	Write your negative thought(s) here. (Hot Thoughts) *What was I thinking when this happened?*	Describe how you felt. *How did I feel when this happened?* (Pro tip: you can feel more than one emotion during a stressful situation, such as scared and disappointed.)	Write down other ways to view the situation or what you may have learned because of the situation.	It's your time to shine! Write down an alternative thought to your Hot Thought based on what you wrote in the previous column. (Pro tip: You can use the Power of YET here, if you want.)	Write down how you feel after writing out your counter-thought, which helps you see the situation in a different way. Did you notice your feelings change when you changed the way you thought about the situation? Great job!

LEVEL UP

SKILLS LEARNED

 Your brain is like a supercomputer that is in charge of EVERYTHING you do.

 The two important parts of the brain that impact your stress and anxiety are:

- The **Prefrontal Cortex (PFC),** which helps you make plans and decisions as well as practice self control, and

- The **Amygdala,** which is the Safety Center of the brain, controls your emotions. Its job is to keep you safe.

 The **Amygdala's** reactions to a perceived threat are the **Fight, Flight, Freeze,** and **Fawn** responses.

Your brain has the ability to change and adapt as a result of new experiences. This is called **neuroplasticity.** This means that with effort and practice you can change your brain!

 Cognitive-behavioral therapy (CBT) is an evidence-based approach that offers strategies to level up your stress management skills.

 Your thoughts are powerful! What **you think** directly impacts how **you feel** and what **you do**.

 A **Hot Thought** is an automatic negative reaction to a perceived threat or problem.

 Mental Hacks learned in this level include practicing the **Power of YET,** and completing a **Thought Record.**

CONGRATULATIONS ON COMPLETING LEVEL 2! YOU'VE CRUSHED ANOTHER LEVEL ON YOUR STRESS MASTERY QUEST. KEEP GOING! SEE YOU IN LEVEL 3.

LEVEL 3

HEALTH CHECK:
EATING, EXERCISING,
AND SLEEPING

*Y*ou're a middle schooler now. There is more expected from you at home and school. Did you know that you need to level up your food game to be able to keep up and take care of your body during stressful times? That's right! A healthy body and brain make it easier to think more clearly, and the way you think impacts everything you do!

REMEMBER THAT YOUR BEHAVIORS (THE THINGS YOU DO EVERY DAY/WEEK) WILL ALSO IMPACT THE WAY YOU THINK AND HOW YOU FEEL.

Let's see what Luna's been up to....Luna has been feeling more tired lately and not performing as well at her field hockey games and tournaments. She's wondering why she used to be able to play a whole game and not feel nearly as worn out as she does now.

Luna can develop a better stress management game plan for field hockey by taking a look at the three parts of stress in this area.

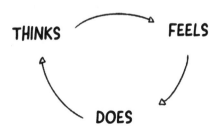

THINKS   FEELS

DOES

When it comes to behaviors, Luna hasn't been eating consistently (she's skipping meals) and when she does eat, she's been eating foods that are unhealthy (high in sugar and fat), which make her feel sluggish throughout the day. Luna also hasn't been practicing in between games like she used to. And she's having trouble sleeping, which makes her tired throughout the day and exhausted on game days. These behaviors then make her feel tired, frustrated, stressed, and disappointed in herself. Because she's developed these habits (**Behaviors**) and is feeling the consequences of these behaviors (**Feelings**), she then has a negative mindset (**Thoughts**) such as:

- I'm lazy.
- I'm not getting better.
- I definitely won't make it on the team for next season.

So what can Luna (and you!) do? First, we come up with a plan to keep your body healthy in order to support your stress management skills like a boss. Let's do this!

WHAT'S ON YOUR PLATE? Good nutrition is important to help you grow, be healthy, and even do better in school! It's helpful to develop healthy habits early, because the habits that you develop now tend to stay with you through your teen and adult life.

The truth is that many middle schoolers have diets that are not balanced, and are high in sugary snacks. Nutritional researchers have found that these poor eating habits are a risk factor for decreased sport performance, low energy levels, academic failure, poor stress management, and depression. You may notice that too many days in a row of eating a lot of unhealthy food or snacks can make you feel really tired and sluggish. This can get in the way of your sleep and ability to focus, which can impact your grades, and cause more stress.

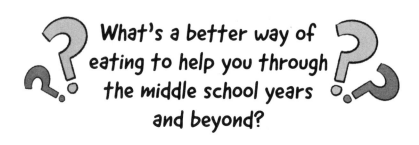

What's a better way of eating to help you through the middle school years and beyond?

Balanced meals that account for healthy dietary guidelines to support development and stress management are a good way to start.

Whole Grains

Whole Grains are considered BRAIN FOOD! It's the #1 energy source for your body.
Examples: Rice, Pasta, Whole Grain Bread, Quinoa, Corn

Protein

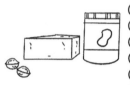

Protein helps your muscles grow! It also helps you feel strong and helps your muscles recover after playing sports. Proteins can be a good source of B vitamins, too.
Examples: Chicken, Pork, Beef, Fish, Seafood, Eggs, Tofu, Beans

Fruit

Fruit is nature's candy! It satisfies your sweet tooth and contains fiber and lots of vitamins to keep you healthy.
Examples: Apples, Bananas, Strawberries, Grapes, Blueberries, Blackberries, Mangoes, Pineapple

Vegetables

Eat veggies every day! Vegetables are loaded with potassium and calcium, and contain fiber, which supports digestion and helps you feel full.
Examples: Spinach, Lettuce, Kale, Broccoli, Cauliflower, Green Beans, Asparagus

Dairy

Dairy foods contain Vitamin D, Vitamin B12, calcium, and potassium. These foods support a healthy immune system and the development of strong bones and muscles.
Examples: Cheese, Yogurt, Milk, Cottage cheese

HEALTHY FOODS HAVE STRESS-BUSTING SUPERPOWERS! When you're feeling stressed or really down, it's really important to focus on drinking enough water and eating a lot of fruits, vegetables, and unprocessed foods. It's helpful to see the foods that you put on your plate as both medicine and stress-busters.

Remember that the key to level up your healthy plate game is to eat in a balanced way that includes a variety of foods that are good for you. Too much bread and dairy products, which are typically highly processed foods, can cause inflammation in your body. **Inflammation** in your body can make you feel tired as well as weaken your immune system. **Processed food** means that the food has been cooked, canned, frozen, packaged, or changed in nutritional composition by being fortified, preserved, or prepared in different ways. The most heavily processed foods often are pre-made meals, like chips, cookies, sugary cereals, frozen pizza, and microwaveable meals. The goal is to eat food that has lots of nutrients, and meals with healthy ingredients.

VITAMIN D	Vitamin D is good for your bones. Vitamin D is also important for a healthy immune system, teeth, muscle power, and strength.
VITAMIN B12	Vitamin B12 is also good for your bones, plus it supports healthy hair, skin, and nails. B12 is good for your brain and helps improve your mood and ability to remember things. It can give you an energy boost, too!
VITAMIN C	Vitamin C is essential for healthy bones, teeth, and gums. Vitamin C also helps your body heal quickly when you're sick, as it helps your immune system keep you healthy. This powerful vitamin helps your brain function better, too!
CALCIUM	Calcium is super important as it helps your body circulate blood and move your muscles. It is also important for healthy teeth and keeps your bones strong!
POTASSIUM	Potassium supports your kidney function and helps your heart get strong. Also, it's important for a healthy immune system.
MAGNESIUM	Magnesium is a mineral that's crucial for your brain and body to function. Magnesium helps keep your blood pressure normal, bones strong, and heart healthy. Magnesium can even boost your athletic performance because it converts food into energy. Additionally, magnesium helps combat low mood and anxiety by reducing inflammation in your body. It can also help you sleep better at night. Magnesium for the win!

Once you've learned the importance of each food group and the vitamins they have, it's time to get them all on your plate!

A Healthy Plate

HEALTHY OILS

VEGETABLES

WHOLE GRAINS

WATER

DAIRY

STAY ACTIVE

FRUITS

HEALTHY PROTEIN

As you can see, a healthy plate has four sections: **fruits, vegetables, whole grains,** and **healthy proteins** as well as **dairy** and **water** to drink.

If you look closely, you will see that:

- Fruits and vegetables should take up half of the plate.

- Grains and proteins take about one-quarter (25% each) of the plate.

The plate is divided this way to help you keep your portion sizes in check and give you an idea on how to balance your meal. This model plate can be used for breakfast, lunch, or dinner.

Of course, every meal might not look perfect every day. You might not eat a lot of vegetables for breakfast most days! The goal is to eat a variety of food groups at each meal. If you don't include veggies in your breakfast plate, then consider a veggie snack (for example, baby carrots with hummus, yum!) in the afternoon, or extra veggies during your dinner to make up for it.

LET'S EAT THE RAINBOW! "Eat the rainbow" is a phrase that nutrition experts use to help you remember to include more nutritious fruits and veggies in your meals. Those foods are really colorful! It's a handy reminder because these "colorful foods" have different benefits for your body and brain.

- **Blue**berries and **red** bell peppers contain vitamins, fiber, and many other nutrients that support healthy growth and help prevent problems such as obesity and dental cavities.

- **Orange**s are full of vitamins C and A, which support healthy joints and eyesight.

- Leafy **green**s such as spinach and lettuce, and green produce like asparagus and avocado, are high in magnesium, vitamins B, K, and E, which improve digestion and support healthy bones.

- **Purple** produce like eggplants and grapes are high in vitamins C and K, which help with memory and support a healthy heart.

Pick colorful foods when you can and focus on the rainbow when selecting fruits and vegetables for the week. The more color, the better! Check out this list for more foods and snack ideas from each color of the rainbow. Notice the health benefits—who knew yellow foods were good for your eyes?

BENEFITS OF EATING THE RAINBOW

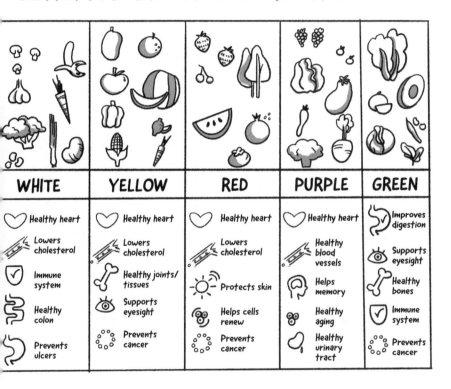

WHITE	YELLOW	RED	PURPLE	GREEN
Healthy heart	Healthy heart	Healthy heart	Healthy heart	Improves digestion
Lowers cholesterol	Lowers cholesterol	Lowers cholesterol	Healthy blood vessels	Supports eyesight
Immune system	Healthy joints/ tissues	Protects skin	Helps memory	Healthy bones
Healthy colon	Supports eyesight	Helps cells renew	Healthy aging	Immune system
Prevents ulcers	Prevents cancer	Prevents cancer	Healthy urinary tract	Prevents cancer

QUEST

MAKE A HEALTHY PLATE

Grab a pencil and paper and draw a plate just like the one on page 68, then build your own healthy plate to level up your stress-busting superpowers!

REMEMBER:

- Make it as colorful as possible (think **Eat the Rainbow**)

- Include **whole grains**

- Avoid fatty proteins—for example, instead of fried chicken, choose grilled chicken. That way your protein selection has less fat and will help you feel energized throughout the day!

MOVEMENT FOR THE WIN!

The Centers for Disease Control and Prevention (CDC) explains that regular physical activity helps kids improve heart health, build strong bones and muscles, control their weight, and reduce symptoms of anxiety and depression. That's a lot of benefits just from moving your body every day! I call physical activity, "**Movement**," because I notice that when I'm coaching middle schoolers just like you, the word "exercise" can sound intimidating. You might feel like in order to work on your physical activity goals, you need to become a full-blown athlete, when that's not the case at all. So your goal for this level is **moving your body**. When your body is sedentary (meaning long periods of sitting or lying down) it has a big impact on your mood, energy levels, and even your brain! You might have experienced that you feel sluggish after sitting on the couch all afternoon playing video games or bingeing Netflix. It's all because you didn't get enough movement during that day.

How much is <u>enough</u> movement?

The US Department of Health and Human Services recommends that middle schoolers engage in at least **60 minutes of moderate or vigorous movement every day**. This means movement that gets your blood pumping and your body sweating. Don't worry, you don't have to do it all at once. For example, participating in gym class and riding your bike after school both count towards your movement goals for the day.

GET MOVING!

Low-to-Moderate intensity movement for as little as 30 minutes a day can be a great way to start! This can be things like:

- Going on a walk with a family member or friend
- Climbing stairs
- Dancing in your room
- Home workouts that you can find on YouTube—for example:

  - Yoga for Teens | *Yoga with Adriene*
  - Rainbow Yoga | Yoga for All Ages! | *Yoga with Adriene*
  - 8-Minute Workout for Teens (Back-to-School) | No Equipment | *Joanna Soh*

  - Wake Up – Fresh Start Fitness | *GoNoodle*
  - Pump it Up – Fresh Start Fitness | *GoNoodle*

Aerobic movement activities make your heart rate increase. **It's important to remember to stay hydrated by drinking water during these activities.** Also remember to drink water after you're done to help your body recover successfully.

Examples include:

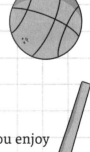

Running	Roller skating or rollerblading
Swimming	Gymnastics
Riding your bike	Hiking
Jumping rope	Soccer
Playing at the park with family or friends	Tag games
Dancing	Playing a sport you enjoy
Brisk walking (a quicker pace than regular walking)	

QUEST

MY MOVEMENT PLAN

Grab a pen and paper and write down 2–4 examples of movement activities that you want to practice as part of your healthy body routine. Then, use a calendar like this one to schedule your movement plan for the week. You got this!

MONDAY	TUESDAY	WEDNESDAY	THURSDAY
Movement Plan: Go for a walk around my neighborhood after school	Movement Plan: Ride my bike after school	Movement Plan: Youtube workout	Movement Plan: Go for a swim with a friend

FRIDAY	SATURDAY	SUNDAY
Movement Plan: Soccer practice	Movement Plan: Soccer game	Movement Plan: Yoga before bed

IT'S ALL ABOUT THE ZZZs

Let's level up your Sleep Routine. You've probably heard it before, but sleep is a very important part of your daily habits. Why? Because you benefit a lot from getting the right amount and quality sleep each night. Let's check out these benefits.

SLEEP SUPERPOWERS

Sleep is necessary to be able to level up your stress management skills and decrease anxiety. A recent study showed that people who don't get enough sleep have trouble fighting stressful sticky thoughts like: "I'll never be able to get this math problem." "Why didn't my friend text me back??" "I never have time to see my friends." "I have so much homework to do!"

GETTING YOUR ZZZs WILL BOOST YOUR IMMUNE SYSTEM. When you are well-rested, your body is able to fight off sickness more effectively. Also, according to the American Academy of Sleep Medicine, a good bedtime routine and a good night's rest can also make vaccines more effective, a definite plus!

GETTING YOUR ZZZs WILL HELP YOU FIGHT JUNK FOOD CRAVINGS. When you're tired, you are more likely to reach for a candy bar instead of a healthy snack. When you don't sleep enough, you feel more stressed and don't have the energy to fight those pesky junk food cravings. Getting enough sleep has been found to help curb sugar cravings and keep your body from gaining excess weight.

GETTING ENOUGH SLEEP MAKES YOUR HEART STRONGER! Just like your immune system, your heart needs rest to work properly.

SLEEP IMPROVES YOUR MOOD. When you sleep well, you wake up feeling rested, and feeling rested helps keep your energy levels up! When you have enough energy, challenges that come up during the day won't annoy you as much. And when you do get annoyed, it doesn't turn into anger right away, and you're able to recover faster to move on with your day in a positive way.

GOOD SLEEPING HABITS INCREASE YOUR ABILITY TO BE PRODUCTIVE. This superpower is a win for school! Good sleep helps you experience **better concentration**. And when you have better concentration, your brain is working better when you need it the most! Another superpower that is crucial to level up your academic skills is that good sleep will **improve your memory.** When you sleep, your brain is still working hard, processing and strengthening all the memories you collected throughout the day. Thank you, brain!

SLEEP INCREASES YOUR EXERCISE PERFORMANCE. This one's for your movement goals! In a research study about the effects of poor sleep on basketball players, researchers found that when the players didn't get good sleep, they didn't perform as well on the court the next day. In fact, sleep impacts all types of physical performance. When you sleep enough, your body is able to recover from physical activity and effectively support your:

- Hand-eye coordination
- Reaction time
- Muscle recovery
- Overall energy

Now that you know the great benefits of sleep, let's talk about improving your sleep habits.

When it comes to sleeping, your nightly routine is called **sleep hygiene**. To have healthy sleep hygiene, you need to have both a restful sleep environment and daily routines that help you have consistent and uninterrupted sleep.

Healthy sleep hygiene requires that you:

- Keep a consistent sleep schedule (going to bed and waking up at approximately the same time every day);
- Make your bedroom as comfortable as possible and free of disruptions;

- Follow a relaxing wind-down plan; and
- Build healthy habits during the day that help you level up your sleep game.

How many hours of sleep do you actually need?

The American Academy of Sleep Medicine recommends that middle schoolers regularly **sleep 9–12 hours per day.** When you sleep between 9–12 hours per day, you get to benefit from all those sleep superpowers we just discussed.

LET'S LEVEL UP YOUR SLEEP HYGIENE SKILLS!
Here's how:

1. Make it a daily priority to get enough sleep.

2. Have a consistent nightly routine. Here are some tips:

   - Try to go to sleep and wake up at the same time every day, even on weekends. When you sleep in on the weekends, make sure you wake up within two hours of your weekday wake-up time.

- Avoid taking naps during the day, because this can make it harder to fall asleep at night.

- Set an alarm clock for the morning wake-up time. You can even set your alarm to play your favorite song to wake up calm, energized, and in a good mood!

- Before bedtime, do things you find relaxing to help you wind down from the day, like taking a relaxing bath, listening to calming music, or reading a book you like.

- Consider listening to a relaxation app like Smiling Mind—check out the Sleep for Teens program or the Feeling It program (with a dark screen).

- Try not to use a phone or any screen for an hour before bed. If you are using a relaxation app, keep it on dark mode.

- Make sure your room is as comfortable as possible and is not too cold or too hot.

- Dim the lights or use a nightlight when it's getting close to bedtime to adjust your eyes and prepare your body for rest.

It's important to make sure you're meeting your movement goals for the day. However, don't do very strenuous exercise close to bedtime because this may keep you up. When it comes to food and snacks, avoid drinking caffeine after 12PM. Caffeine is found in sodas, energy drinks, coffee, and some teas. If you're not sure, read the label on the drink and it will tell you if it has caffeine or not. Avoid eating a huge meal for dinner. A small and light snack before bed is a good idea. Calming tea like chamomile or valerian root can help you relax, too.

Your bed is for sleeping! Do your homework or watch shows somewhere else.

3. Find another place to do your homework or watch YouTube! It's recommended for you to keep electronics or TVs outside the bedroom anyway, so find a desk or table outside the bedroom to charge your tech or do your schoolwork on.

Here's a visual to remind you what to do:

Turn off your device 60 minutes before bedtime. Keep your phone on silent or sleep mode or put it in another room.

Go to bed at the same time every night and get up at the same time every day. Set your alarm before bedtime. If you're having trouble sleeping, don't stare at the clock or tell yourself "GO TO SLEEP!"

Do something calming like read or listen to quiet music 30 minutes before bedtime.

SLEEP PROBLEMS HAPPEN TO EVERYONE! You may need to level up your sleep hygiene if:

- You're having trouble with anxious or unwanted thoughts
- You're having trouble falling asleep or waking up in the morning
- You've been feeling irritable and you're not sure why
- You've been feeling overly emotional and moody
- You've been feeling restless
- You're having trouble concentrating in school
- You're having trouble staying awake at school

If more than one of the scenarios on that list sound like you, that's a good indicator that you should level up your sleep hygiene. Let's do it!

 **How can I improve my sleep hygiene?**

QUEST

IMPROVING MY SLEEP HYGIENE

Grab a piece of paper and a pen. Use examples from Luna's nightly routine or any of the sleep tips you've learned in this chapter, and pick some that you can add to your bedtime routine. Try them for a week, and see how you benefit from all the sleep superpowers! At the end of the week, check in with yourself and consider; has my sleep hygiene improved?

Now let's check in on Luna to see how her stress cycle changed after leveling up her Healthy Plate, Movement Plan, and Sleep Hygiene:

LUNA THINKS

- I feel more energized during practice and can keep up during games.
- My technique on the field is improving!
- I'm confident that I'll get better with practice.

LUNA FEELS

- More confident in her skills as a field hockey player.
- Full of energy and strong during and after games.

LUNA DOES

- Practices between games as one of her movement goals.
- Eats the rainbow—her meals are healthy and very colorful!
- Keeps healthy protein snacks in her backpack for days when she doesn't have a lot of time to eat.
- Sleeps 10 hours every night and feels rested when she wakes up.

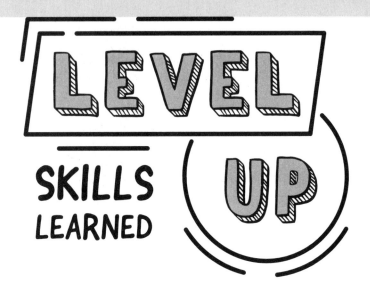

LEVEL UP

SKILLS LEARNED

 Your **behaviors** (the things you do every day/week) will impact the way you think and how you feel.

 Good nutrition is important to help you grow, be healthy, and support you doing better in school!

 Your **Healthy Plate** should include the five food groups: **whole grains, protein, fruit, vegetables**, **dairy,** and of course, plenty of **water!**

 Fruits and vegetables should take up half (50%) of your healthy plate, and grains and proteins will take about one-quarter (25%) each of your plate.

Eat the Rainbow! Colorful foods have special benefits for your health and body. Choose vegetables and fruits of all different colors for your healthy plate.

 Move your body every day! The goal is **60 minutes of moderate or vigorous movement every day**, so go ahead and get your sweat on!

 Sleep is a game changer! Sleeping well and having a consistent bedtime routine boosts your immune system and keeps your body, brain, and heart strong. Sleep also helps you concentrate better in school and remember things that you study.

CONGRATULATIONS ON COMPLETING LEVEL 3! FEEL PROUD OF HOW FAR YOU'VE COME. CAN'T WAIT TO CONQUER LEVEL 4 WITH YOU!

CHILL-OUT HACKS

ou've done a great job so far learning the strategies needed to level up your stress management skills. Now it's time to put all that knowledge into practice. Let's learn more about the tools you can use to put your current level up skills to the test and really step up your stress-busting game!

Ever have trouble passing a video game level and need a little extra help? Sometimes all you need is to learn a special trick or hack to accomplish your goal. Now that you know how your brain works and what your body needs to handle stress better, you can benefit from some tricks to get you to the next level. In this chapter, you'll learn how to help yourself chill out or feel more relaxed, so worries won't get in the way. I call these helpful tricks your **Chill-Out Hacks.**

REMEMBER THE STRESS CYCLE? In Level 2 you learned that feeling stressed impacts the way you think, how you feel, and what you do. So, it's important to have skills that help you feel better in the moments when stress tries to take over. These **Chill-Out Hacks** have been researched and are proven to help you feel calmer and regain control of your body and your brain when you need it the most.

THERE ARE TWO MAIN CATEGORIES OF CHILL-OUT HACKS, WHICH HELP YOU MANAGE THE STRESS CYCLE IN SPECIFIC WAYS:

PHYSICAL (→ YOU DO) and **MENTAL** (→ YOU THINK). There are a whole bunch of hacks to learn, and you may find some work better for you than others.

PHYSICAL CHILL-OUT HACKS

Have you ever been so frustrated that you felt like you wanted to hit something? That feeling is excess energy that's stuck in your body wanting to come out. It's important that you use up this energy in a helpful rather than an unhelpful or unsafe way so that you can bring your body and your brain back to a calm state. This is where **Physical Chill-out Hacks,** like movement and stretching, come in.

Physical Chill-Out Hacks will help you use up that stuck energy in a safe and useful way to support you feeling calm and more in control. In the last chapter you learned all about how movement supports your ability to think more clearly, focus, and relieve stress. With these great benefits of movement in mind, you can use the following strategies to help you chill out when you need to.

PROGRESSIVE MUSCLE RELAXATION (PMR) is simple to practice and very beneficial to support calming your body during stressful times. This technique involves tensing, or tightening, one muscle group at a time, then letting go of all the tension to create a relaxed state. To practice PMR, you will tense and relax each muscle group one at a time, in a specific order. This is one of Otto's favorite chill-out hacks, so watch him show you how it's done.

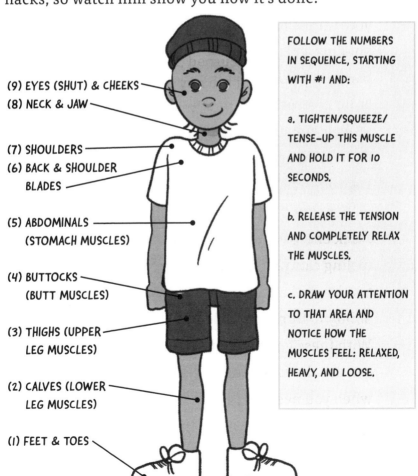

(9) EYES (SHUT) & CHEEKS

(8) NECK & JAW

(7) SHOULDERS

(6) BACK & SHOULDER BLADES

(5) ABDOMINALS (STOMACH MUSCLES)

(4) BUTTOCKS (BUTT MUSCLES)

(3) THIGHS (UPPER LEG MUSCLES)

(2) CALVES (LOWER LEG MUSCLES)

(1) FEET & TOES

FOLLOW THE NUMBERS IN SEQUENCE, STARTING WITH #1 AND:

a. TIGHTEN/SQUEEZE/ TENSE-UP THIS MUSCLE AND HOLD IT FOR 10 SECONDS.

b. RELEASE THE TENSION AND COMPLETELY RELAX THE MUSCLES.

c. DRAW YOUR ATTENTION TO THAT AREA AND NOTICE HOW THE MUSCLES FEEL: RELAXED, HEAVY, AND LOOSE.

PMR is great for when you need to chill out quickly and need a discreet strategy (since you can do it without others even noticing!). Otto sometimes uses a stress ball when he's practicing PMR, but you don't need one to use this strategy successfully.

GET OUTSIDE AND WALK IT OUT! Just going for a walk sounds too easy, doesn't it? Here's the thing: when you are feeling stressed or stuck with all this extra energy, you can use your body to regain a sense of control and come back to a calm state. This is not only a physical chill-out hack but also a **Mental Hack**, or trick that helps you change the way your brain is responding to stress.

Remember how your brain is a supercomputer? Well, moving your body and changing your environment, even for a brief moment, allows you to reboot your brain and think more clearly. Research shows that worries are part of an **Automatic System** in your body, meaning that sometimes you can't control it. So, when your brain is feeling stuck with worry thoughts, for example, you can benefit from focusing on a **Mechanical System** in your body (or one that you can totally control) to change the way you feel quickly. A system in your body that you have total control over is physical movement! This means that even though sometimes you can't control what you are thinking about or how stuck you feel on a thought, you can always control whether you move your body intentionally. This is why going for a walk is a game-changer when it comes to calming your body down. **Going for a walk** helps in two ways: it changes your environment *and* provides the benefits of physical movement to help you feel better quickly.

You don't need a long walk to be able to calm your body down. If you're at school, you might just need to take a break to walk to the bathroom and get a drink of water. When you're at home and feeling stuck on a math problem, going outside to get some fresh air and give yourself a break will help you move your body and help you relax. Then you'll be ready to take on that math problem with more energy and a fresh perspective.

SOMETIMES YOU CAN'T CONTROL YOUR WORRIES BECAUSE THEY HAPPEN AUTOMATICALLY. BUT YOU CAN ALWAYS OVERRIDE THIS RESPONSE BY MOVING YOUR BODY. REMEMBER, YOU—NOT

YOUR WORRIES—ARE THE BOSS OF YOUR BRAIN! BUT WAIT—THERE ARE MORE PHYSICAL CHILL-OUT HACKS! These involve movement, stretching, yoga poses, and breathing. First, let's try Wall Presses and Running in Place.

Wall Presses are exactly what they sound like:

- Face a wall and press your palms against the wall.
- Bend your elbows and lean into the wall slowly while counting to three.
- Hold that position for one second.
- Slowly push back while counting to three, straightening your arms.
- Repeat this pattern five times. It's kind of like doing push-ups against the wall!

Same with **Running in Place.** All you do is:

- Run in place for 30 seconds.

- Take a brief break to catch your breath.

- Run in place again for 60 seconds.

- Check in with how you're feeling...still not feeling calm? You can try to run in place for another 30 seconds until you're feeling better.

Next up are a few empowering stretching movements to try. Figure out which ones you like best by first giving them all a try.

Power Up Pose (MOUNTAIN POSE)

is a stretching movement. You can do it right before the next two calming stretches—Catch the Wave and Child Pose. **Mountain Pose** will help you feel grounded before completing your other calming stretches. When your thoughts are racing and stress is taking over, standing tall and grounding yourself helps you regain a calm and powerful feeling all over your body. When you feel grounded, you feel stable and present. Here's how to do the Power Up Pose:

- Stand with your feet about hip-width apart (this means your feet and legs are positioned straight down, right under your hips).
- Put your arms to your sides, position your hands with your palms forward and your fingers spread apart.
- Roll your shoulders back and stand straight.
- Relax your shoulders toward the ground (level and not pulled up into a shrug position).
- Imagine you're a mountain and slowly breathe in through your nose for 4 seconds and out through your mouth for 4 seconds five times in a row. Notice anything different? Perhaps you're feeling calmer and more centered.

Catch the Wave (WARRIOR 1 POSE).

Begin in Power Up Pose and pretend you're standing on a surfboard.

- Take a deep breath in and when you exhale, step your left foot to the back of the imaginary surfboard. Straighten and extend your left foot so it feels comfortable. Make sure both heels follow one straight line.

- Point your right foot towards the front of the surfboard, and turn your head to follow it.

- Bend your right knee so that it comes directly over the top of your right ankle and straighten your back leg.

- Extend your arms straight out over your legs creating a straight line.

- Relax your shoulders and breathe gently in through your nose and out through your mouth a couple of times while you catch some imaginary waves.

- Repeat all instructions with opposite legs to stretch both sides!

Cool Down (CHILD'S) Pose. Here's how you do it.

- Kneel on the floor with your toes together and your knees hip-width apart.
- Breathe in through your nose and on your exhale, lower your chest to the ground in between your knees.
- Stretch out your arms in front of you with your palms facing down and forehead touching the ground.
- Relax your shoulders towards the floor.
- Rest in this pose and breathe slowly in through your nose and out through your mouth until your body starts to feel calm.

IF YOU'D LIKE TO LEARN MORE STRETCHES LIKE THESE TO ADD TO YOUR CHILL-OUT HACK LIST, MAKE SURE TO CHECK OUT THE RESOURCE LIST AT THE END OF THE BOOK!

BREATHING CHILL-OUT HACKS. You've probably heard a supportive caregiver or friend tell you to take a deep breath when you're feeling worked up. Ever wonder why? Well, research shows that breathing in a specific way benefits your body and brain in many ways, including helping you calm down.

Biologically speaking, when you are stressed or anxious, your brain releases a stress hormone called cortisol into your bloodstream. Cortisol is the stress hormone that makes your heart feel like it's racing, your palms sweaty, and your muscles tense up. By taking deep breaths, more oxygen enters your body and helps your heart rate slow down, overriding the effects of cortisol. When your heart rate slows down, your brain receives the message that you are OK, safe, and ready to relax.

Deep breathing also increases endorphins in your body. Endorphins are feel-good chemicals that your brain produces. That means that when your brain produces endorphins, you feel good! Endorphins are released by your brain during physical activity (movement) and deep breathing, which means both these activities improve your mood, increase your energy levels, and can even help you sleep better.

THE MORE ENDORPHINS YOUR BRAIN MAKES, THE BETTER YOU FEEL. YOUR BRAIN MAKES ENDORPHINS WHEN YOU MOVE YOUR BODY AND TAKE DEEP BREATHS!

You may be thinking, "but I breathe all day and I don't feel calm all the time!" Good point, but here's the thing: you breathe without thinking and can actually be breathing in a shallow way, meaning that you are not taking in as much oxygen as your body may need. Many people breathe in a way that doesn't support them feeling calm, without even realizing it. The following breathing techniques will require you to breathe in a deep and intentional way (while paying attention) to get the full benefit from those positive effects. Knowing what breathing technique works best for you will be a great tool to have as you level up your stress management skills.

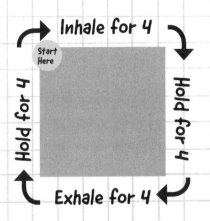

Inhale for 4

Hold for 4 (left side)

Hold for 4 (right side)

Exhale for 4

Start Here

Square (4 X 4) Breathing. You can do square breathing anywhere, standing or sitting. Use this guide to follow along.

- Slowly exhale all of the air out of your lungs.
- Take a deep breath in through your nose and blow all the air out through your mouth like you're blowing out a birthday candle.
- Imagine a square, or use the one provided above.
- Inhale through your nose slowly for the count of four, as you imagine using your finger to across the top of the square.
- Next, trace down the side of the square while holding your breath for a count of four.
- Trace across the bottom of the square and gently exhale through your mouth for a count of four.
- Finish tracing up the side of the square as you pause and hold your breath for the count of four once more.
- Repeat five times or until you're feeling calmer.

Handy Breathing.

You can do handy breathing anywhere, standing or sitting, and all you need are your hands and a few seconds of your time!

For this **Chill-Out Hack,** you take five slow breaths by tracing your hand. Handy, right?!

Spread one hand open and stretch out your fingers. You can use your right or left hand.

- Take the pointer finger of your other hand and start by placing it at the bottom of the thumb of your spread-out hand.
- Trace your finger up your thumb and breathe in through your nose, pause at the tip of your thumb, then slowly breathe out through your mouth as you trace all the way down.
- Breathe in through your nose once more as you trace up your second finger and breathe out through your mouth as you trace down.
- Remember to breathe in and out slowly while you trace your hand so you can get the full benefit from this calm-down technique.
- Keep going until you have finished tracing all your fingers and completed your five chill-out breaths.
- Repeat as needed until you're feeling calm and relaxed.

Here's another kind of breathing you can do just about anywhere, standing, sitting, or even lying down. It's called **4-7-8 Breathing.** Check it out:

- Begin by slowly exhaling all of the air out of your lungs. Take a deep breath in through your nose and blow all the air out with your mouth like you're trying to cool a cup of hot cocoa.
- Place the tip of your tongue on your gums behind your front teeth.
- Breathe in slowly through your nose for four seconds and make sure your belly is expanding when your breathe in.
- Hold your breath for a count of seven seconds.
- Exhale through your mouth making a whoosh sound to the count of eight seconds.
- Repeat five times or until feeling calmer.

MENTAL HACKS

Remember in Level 2 when you learned all about your amazing brain? To recap, when feeling stressed, a part of your brain called the **amygdala** takes charge because its most important job is to keep you safe. When this happens, you temporarily lose access to the "smart parts" of your brain like the **cerebrum** and **PFC**. It's like they go offline for a minute. This happens because your brain's most important job when you're stressed is to keep you safe and engage in the **Fight, Flight, Freeze, or Fawn** stress responses. Mental Hacks are tricks or cognitive strategies you can use to override your brain's safety response and bring all the parts of your brain back online so you can think clearly and feel calm.

ABC LISTS. Bet you didn't think the alphabet would come in handy when managing your stress response! This strategy works so well because you need your whole brain in order to come up with the list, so it really helps bring all the parts of your brain back online. This Mental Hack can be done on your own or with a friend or caregiver, by making it into a game and taking turns.

Ready? Here's how to do the ABC List.

- Pick a topic such as types of food (fruits, sweet treats, veggies), places (countries, cities, make-believe lands), animals, people names, or sports. Whatever category you want!

- Think of something in that category that starts with the letter A. Then move on to the next letters. For example, A is for Apple, B is for Banana, C is for Cucumber, etc.

- Try to list as many items as you can think of until you're feeling calm and can think more clearly.

PICTURE IT. This is kind of like daydreaming in real-time. Just focus your mind on calming and serene images and experiences. Remember **what you think, you feel, and do**? By picturing a relaxing scene in your mind, you will feel calm in your body as well. This strategy helps you use your amazing imagination to feel calm and more in control when stress is getting in the way.

- Find a comfortable place to sit or lie down
- Take a few deep breaths to help you relax
- Picture the following scenario in detail

If you need a little help getting started, you can have someone read the script aloud to you or read it yourself and then picture it in your mind. You can also find suggestions at the end of the book for apps that have guided relaxation recordings you can listen to, like Insight Timer.

RELAXING VISUALIZATION SCRIPT: MY HAPPY PLACE

Find a comfortable and quiet place to sit. Close your eyes if you feel comfortable doing so. Focus on your breathing. As you breathe in through your nose and out through your mouth, notice how your chest and your belly move while taking slow, calming breaths. Just listen as smooth, clean air moves in and out of your body. Notice that it's a quiet and calming sound.

- Imagine yourself outside on a beautiful day.

- Picture yourself walking along a path. You can feel the warmth and energy from the sun on your skin. You enjoy your walk along the path on this peacefully sunny day. You are feeling relaxed and happy on your walk.

- Soon you notice a gate in front of you. Picture the gate coming up ahead. What does it look like? You walk up to the gate, and beyond it you can see a special garden that makes you feel happy, safe, and comfortable. Excitedly, you push the gate doors open, walk in, and enter your own private space.

- Take a good look all around you. All your favorite things are here waiting for you. Take your time noticing all the colors and shapes that surround you now. What colors and shapes do you see? Notice how beautiful your garden is. This garden is your calm and happy place.

- As you continue to look around, notice how things feel here. Perhaps some things are soft and warm, and others are smooth and cool. Does the air feel warm or cold on your skin? Spend some time exploring, using your sense of touch as you continue to feel comfortable and at peace here.

- Listen to the sounds that you hear around you. The sounds you hear are enjoyable and comforting to you. Do you hear music? Or maybe it's quiet in your garden? Are birds singing? Some of the sounds may be soft, while others may be louder. What do you hear? Relax and listen for a while and see if you can identify the different sounds in your garden.

- Take a deep breath in and notice the smells that are present. Some of them may be familiar, while others may be new smells. Focus on your sense of smell and notice that the fragrance is pleasant and soothing.

- Take your time and enjoy your special place. Notice how happy, calm, and at peace you feel here surrounded by all your favorite things.

- When you are ready to leave, slowly walk back towards the gate and feel how calm and relaxed you feel now that you've spent some time in your happy place. These feelings will stay with you throughout the day. Push the gate open and return to the path you started on today.

- As you make your way back up the path, remember that you can come back whenever you need to. Visit your happy place any time you would like to relax and feel calm. You are now ready to return to your day. Gently stretch your arms and legs, wiggle your toes and fingers, and finally, open your eyes feeling refreshed and ready to take on what's next in your day.

Quest

CHILL-OUT HACK

Alright, time for another quest. This time you'll be working on your own Chill-Out Hack plan. Pick one Physical, Breathing, or Mental Chill-Out Hack to practice once a day, every day this week. Why every day? Well, to really make the best use of your Chill-Out Hacks, you need to practice using them consistently BEFORE you need them the most, when you're feeling stressed. Research shows that it's helpful to take some time every day to practice how to chill so that you're better able to use these skills during stressful times.

Grab a piece of paper and something to write with. Now, write down one chill-out hack you'd like to practice using starting today. It's helpful to choose a consistent time of day to practice your chill-out hack, so you'll remember and develop the habit quicker. You can also use an app to help you track your practice and help you build healthy habits (there are some suggestions in the resource list at the end of the book).

NEED SOME INSPIRATION? CHECK OUT THE PLAYERS' CHILL-OUT HACKS.

Luna decided that she will practice **PMR** before bed.

Rowan will use the **Picture It Mental Hack** before doing their afternoon responsibilities (chores, homework, etc.) to feel more calm and relaxed.

Otto will practice **Square Breathing or 4-7-8 Breathing** on the bus to school so he starts off his day making sure all the smart parts of his brain are online and ready to go!

 **WHAT'S YOUR CHILL-OUT PLAN?**

Copy the text below and fill it out. Place it somewhere you can see it to remind yourself to follow your chill-out plan.

I will practice _____

every day this week at this time _____

as part of my chill-out plan.

IF A CHILL-OUT HACK DOESN'T WORK FOR YOU, THAT'S OK! TRY A DIFFERENT ONE NEXT TIME AND SEE HOW THAT MAKES YOU FEEL. YOU HAVE OPTIONS!

You now have some strategies to help you when you're feeling stressed! Remember to try different ones out to figure out which work best for you. Next, we'll learn an additional way to use your amazing brain and in particular, your attention, to help you feel calm and relaxed when you're stressed. Let's talk about **Mindfulness.**

MIND FULL OR MINDFUL?

Do you ever notice that your mind can think about lots of things at once?

Did I pack all my field hockey gear?

What am I having for lunch today?

Is that quiz happening today?

Why didn't my friend text me back last night?

I need to wish Rowan good luck with their speech later!

Like all of us, Luna's brain is sometimes flooded with many different thoughts. When your mind is **full** in this way, it can make you feel scattered and stressed. What if I told you there was a special way you could use your brain to pay attention to things in a way that will help you feel relaxed and more in control? Well, there is, and it's called **Mindfulness**. Mindfulness is a way to supercharge your attention skills. Mindfulness is all about paying attention to what's happening right now (in the present moment). It means really noticing what you are experiencing, and because you are paying attention in this way, you are better able to support your mood and emotions. Mindfulness skills also help you better notice the way you are feeling, what you are thinking about, and what you are doing. When you are able to observe yourself in this way, you can more easily make choices that will help you relax and calm down.

MINDFULNESS IS A SUPERPOWER! Research shows that practicing mindfulness regularly helps you:

- Regulate emotions,
- Improve focus and concentration,
- Plan and organize,
- Increase your self-control, and even helps you
- Get better grades.

Like all skills, mindfulness takes practice. But there are lots of ways to do it! Some of them even combine physical and mental chill-out hacks. Let's check some of them out:

5-SENSES GROUNDING. This Mindfulness Mental Hack is simple. You can do it on your own and in any setting you're in. All you need is yourself and your hand to keep you on track. You will be using your five senses (seeing, hearing, touching, smelling, and tasting) to bring your attention back to the present moment. When you feel your mind is full and need to practice some mindfulness, just do the following:

- Take a moment to look around you and identify:
  - ☐ 5 things you can see
  - ☐ 4 things you can feel
  - ☐ 3 things you can hear
  - ☐ 2 things you can smell
  - ☐ 1 thing that you would like to taste
- Slow down your thoughts and use all your senses to focus on and fully experience the things you notice.
- With your mind, make a list of the five things you see. Notice the color of the walls in front of you, or the precise shape of an object in the room you are in. Take your time to really *look* and acknowledge what you see.
- Find four things you can touch. For example, the smooth texture of your desk or the softness of your shirt and how it feels against your skin. If you like, spend a moment literally touching these things. Notice if it has a particular texture (hard, soft, smooth, bumpy, rough, etc.) and temperature (cold vs. warm).
- Listen for three sounds that you hear. How would you describe those sounds (loud, quiet, enjoyable, distant)?

- Inhale or sniff an object to identify two smells you can sense. What kind of smell is it (sweet, faint, strong, familiar)?

- Think about your favorite snack; how does it taste (sweet or sour, chewy or crunchy)?

MINDFUL SNACK. Ever grab your favorite snack and look down to realize that you're done eating and just want some more? You then realize you can't really remember eating it, you just know you don't have any more to snack on? This Mindful Snack strategy helps you slow down and pay attention in order to appreciate your food and all its characteristics. This is a delicious practice that can also help you feel calmer and supercharge your mindful attention skills.

- Grab your favorite healthy snack, like some popcorn, raisins, or a piece of fruit.

- Place it in front of you but don't eat it just yet.

- Look at your snack and think about the following:

  ☐ What is its shape?

  ☐ What size is it?

  ☐ What color is it?

- Now pick up your snack with your hand and consider the following:
    - ☐ What does it feel like in your hand?
    - ☐ Does it have a temperature to it (hot or cold)?
    - ☐ Does it have a particular texture (smooth or rough)?
- Next, smell your snack.
    - ☐ What does it smell like?
- Now it's time to place your snack in your mouth (if it's too big to place in your mouth just place a small piece of it in your mouth), let it rest on your tongue, but don't chew it yet!
    - ☐ What does it feel like on your tongue?
    - ☐ What happens in your mouth when you just keep it there without chewing?
- Go ahead and bite down on it, but don't swallow it just yet!
    - ☐ What does it taste like?
    - ☐ Does it taste any different than the other times you've had it before?
- Go ahead and chew your snack slowly and enjoy!
- Notice how you're feeling now that you've had a mindful snack.

MINDFUL WALK. Movement is here to support your stress management and mindfulness skills! Now let's take those supercharged attention skills outside. Going on a mindful walk is a great way to chill and regain a sense of calm when needed. Here's how to go on a Mindful Walk:

- Start your walk and notice how your body is feeling.

- Pay attention to how your legs, feet, and arms feel while you walk. Feel how your feet touch the ground with each step forward.

- As you continue to walk, look around and find one thing you find beautiful that's around you. It can be a type of leaf, a shadow on the sidewalk in front of you, or even a house you walk by.

- Next, focus on your sense of smell and identify some smells you notice along the way. Do you smell fresh cut grass? Or maybe someone is cooking nearby? What do you smell?

- Do you hear anything? Perhaps a neighbor's dog is barking, or the mailman is dropping off packages on the front porch of a house.

- If your mind wanders during your walk, that's OK. Just bring your attention back to your senses and describe what you see, hear, smell, and feel.

TECH SUPPORT. Alright, now that you're equipped with some calming mindfulness strategies, let's add some tech support to your chill-out plan. The following apps are helpful to have and use when you need to chill out. Look for them in your app store or online. If you'd like to learn about more helpful apps like these, make sure to check out the resource list at the of the book!

- **INSIGHT TIMER.** This guided meditations app can guide you through lots of meditations, including progressive muscle relaxation and relaxing visualizations. Try searching for topics like "progressive muscle relaxation," "5 senses grounding," "mindful walk," or even "beach visualization" or "forest visualization."

- **SMILING MIND.** This app also has great mindfulness guided practices that you can use to boost skills learned in this Level. Check out the following programs in the **Youth** section:
  - ☐ Feeling It
  - ☐ Mindfully Back to School
  - ☐ Sleep for Teens

SKILLS LEARNED

 Chill-Out Hacks are helpful strategies that help you feel more relaxed and in control, so worries don't get in the way.

 Physical Chill-Out Hacks involve movement to get rid of excess energy in your body when you're stressed.

 Mental Chill-Out Hacks are cognitive strategies that override your brain's safety response and bring all the parts of your brain back online so you can think clearly, concentrate better, and feel calm.

 Breathing Chill-Out Hacks are special deep breathing techniques that increase how much oxygen enters your body. They help your body relax, increase "feel good" hormones (endorphins), and let your brain know that you are OK and ready to feel calm.

 Mindfulness helps you focus your attention on the present moment to better support your ability to concentrate, your mood and your emotions.

YOUR BRAVERY PLAN

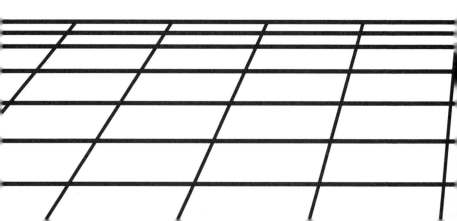

$\mathcal{M}$ iddle school is an academic and social adventure, and an exciting time of discovery. You may have just started middle school, or maybe this is a new school year with brand new teachers to adjust to, new people to meet, and a different way of doing things. Have you ever noticed that every time you start or try something new, fear often comes along for the ride? New experiences can cause you to feel fear. That means you need an antidote or way to conquer that fear, especially as you're leveling up your stress management skills! The antidote to fear is **bravery.**

BRAVERY MEANS DOING SOMETHING EVEN THOUGH YOU CAN'T FEEL BRAVE WITHOUT FEELING SCARED.

Bravery is the admirable personal quality of being able to confront the things that scare you. Often, people think bravery means being fearless. But being brave actually means doing something *even though* you feel scared. If you're never scared, you never have the opportunity to be brave! Bravery can show up in your life in lots of different ways, big and small. It takes *bravery* for a firefighter to go into a burning building to save the people inside, and it also takes *bravery* for someone who is shy to introduce themselves to new classmates at school. Firefighters are often acknowledged for their bravery, but everyday people like you also act bravely every day, when you face your fears.

FEAR AND YOUR FANTASTIC BRAIN

Often, you feel afraid or anxious when facing something new. This makes a lot of sense to your brain. Why? Remember from Level 2 that one of your brain's most important jobs is to keep you safe? Well, your brain is built to feel safe when it **knows what will happen.** When your brain can predict the outcome of a situation, it sends out signals that indicate, "All clear! You're safe and good to go." But when you try something new, it's interpreted as, "Outcome unknown! Safety unknown! Proceed with caution." Trying something new can often be seen as a possible threat to you and your safety, even though it may not be an unsafe situation at all. It's just that your brain can't quite figure out what will happen because it hasn't been taught how to do that yet!

Did you know that fear is often just a sign that you are doing something different than what you're used to?

Fear can also be a good indicator that you are about to learn something new or challenge yourself in some way in order to grow! For example, you may feel stressed because you're not sure whether you've studied enough for your math test tomorrow. You may feel anxious and scared because you **fear** getting a bad grade. You then decide to review your notes or ask a friend to quiz you to make sure you feel ready. In this case, fear came up to encourage you to find ways to feel prepared and ready to take on this academic challenge. Fear helped you grow as a student.

 Has fear ever help you improve in some way?

Like all other skills learned throughout your life, such as your communication, social, math, and reading skills, **Bravery Skills** need to be developed and practiced over time to strengthen. Fear acts like an inner voice that will often tell you *not* to try new things, or to avoid situations that feel scary. You have to challenge this kind of thinking to really build your bravery and stress management skills. Let's focus on *how* to be brave next (and we'll get to making a solid Bravery Plan later in this Level).

An overall formula to being brave is to:

1. Not allow fear to make choices for you.

YOU ARE THE BOSS OF YOUR BRAIN AND YOUR CHOICES, NOT FEAR.

2. Get OK with feeling scared.

IT FEELS UNCOMFORTABLE TO TRY SOMETHING NEW. PUT ON A BRAVE FACE AND REMEMBER THAT THE DISCOMFORT WILL PASS. I PROMISE.

3. Be ready to face your fears head on.

FACE THE THINGS THAT SCARE YOU AND YOU'LL LEARN AND GROW. YOU CAN ACCOMPLISH MORE THAN YOU CAN IMAGINE!

Picture your amazing brain as a powerful ship cruising in the ocean. In order to arrive at its destination, every ship needs an essential crew member: the captain! The captain is knowledgeable about everything the ship does, where the ship needs to go, and how to support the crew during the voyage. The captain of *your* ship should be YOU. But sometimes, when you feel scared... the captain of your ship is actually, **fear**.

Fear bosses you around. When you feel scared, you might think, *I won't be able to do it. This is too hard! Don't try that! It's too scary.* That's fear trying to captain your ship! It's trying to be in charge. Sometimes that inner voice is so strong that it keeps you from trying new things and makes you avoid people, places, and experiences. When this happens, fear is trying to take control (of your thoughts, feelings, and behaviors) and navigate your ship while you're stuck on the shore watching.

Let's make sure you're the captain of your ship! To do that, we need to build your Bravery Skills.

DO NOT ALLOW FEAR TO MAKE CHOICES FOR YOU. To develop your Bravery Skills, you need to take back the captain's seat! You have to decide to not let fear be in control of what you think, feel, and do. Fear cannot be allowed to make choices for you.

To further develop this skill, you need to build up your **Brain Smarts.** What are Brain Smarts? They're your ability to recognize thoughts that are unhelpful and change those thoughts to new thoughts that *will* help you accomplish your goals. There will be more details about Brain Smarts in the next level, but for now let's focus on being in control of what you think (there are a bunch of strategies for changing your thoughts to more helpful ones. You'll see).

GET OK WITH FEELING SCARED. This means learning to roll with it and tolerate the feeling of being afraid. How you feel when you are trying a new sport, introducing yourself to someone, starting a new school, or learning a new skill can all be very uncomfortable at first. The discomfort of trying something new can often make you avoid trying it in the first place. You may notice your body responding in ways that make you feel out of control, such as your heart racing, palms sweating, or having trouble breathing. Sometimes, the discomfort shows up in your thoughts, like when you think, *This is way too hard; I can't do this; I'll never be able to figure this out...*

Whether it shows up in your body or your thoughts, feeling this way is uncomfortable! I get it, feeling uncomfortable is not, well...comfortable. But here's the thing: you don't grow if you don't try new things, and when you try new things your body and brain are built to feel uncomfortable. So you have to learn to be okay with being uncomfortable in order to grow and accomplish personal goals.

Now for the good news: The discomfort you feel when trying something new is *temporary*. This means that it won't last forever. In fact, scientists have determined that when a person reacts to something in their environment, there's a 90-second chemical process that happens in the body, and after that, any remaining emotional response is caused by the person *choosing* to remain in that emotional state. Therefore, experts recommend that when you feel stressed, you should **PAUSE FOR 90 SECONDS AND NAME WHAT YOU ARE FEELING IN THE MOMENT**, like: *I'm scared, I feel angry, I feel frustrated.* This focuses your awareness on your thoughts and feelings, calms your brain down, and helps you regain a sense of calm and control. (Does that sound a little like being Mindful to you? ☺)

 SO, FOR 1.5 MINUTES OF DISCOMFORT, YOU CAN BUILD BRAVERY SKILLS THAT WILL LAST A LIFETIME!

In order to learn to tolerate the uncomfortable feelings that show up when feeling scared, you need to use **Emotion Smarts.** Emotion Smarts are the ability to understand your feelings, how your body reacts to those feelings, and what you need to do to support calming yourself down. In Level 4 you learned all about **Chill-Out Hacks** that help you relax your body when stressed. You'll be using those along with other skills you will learn to build your Emotion Smarts.

When you are fearful of something, it's natural for you to try and avoid it. Your brain and body are built for survival, after all! However, sometimes you are fearful of things just because they are new, different, or difficult to accomplish.

 **BUT WHAT IF YOU FACED THAT FEAR, STEP-BY-STEP?**

Let's see how Luna managed the fear she felt the day before school started.

Luna was looking forward to her first day of school all summer. She was excited to change schools and make new friends. She was also looking forward to joining the field hockey team since her last school didn't have one. The night before school she couldn't sleep. Luna was thinking, *What if I don't know anyone? What if no one talks to me? What if I'm not able to make any friends? What if I get lost in that big new building? What if I don't make the team?* She didn't sleep much that night and, in the morning, when her dad woke her up to get ready for school, she told him she didn't want to go. Her dad explained that it makes sense to feel nervous before the first day of school, especially when it's something brand new, like middle school. He shared with Luna that he feels nervous too before big meetings where he will be presenting. Luna and her dad practiced **4-7-8 Breathing** together. After talking with her dad and doing a Chill-Out Hack, she felt calmer and ready to take on the day.

Turns out that Luna really enjoyed her first day. To be brave, she calmed herself down with a Chill-Out Hack and showed up to school even though she felt scared. She ended up meeting new friends and really connecting with a few of her teachers. She's also excited to try out for the field hockey team soon. The next time she feels nervous about going to school, she will remember her first day jitters, practice a Chill-Out Hack, and tell herself, *I got this! I've done it before, and it all worked out.* Luna successfully faced her fear.

So, following Luna's lead, the last step to build your bravery skills is **Facing Your Fears.** Facing your fears requires preparation, a plan, patience, and practice.

REMEMBER, YOU NEED TO PRACTICE BEING BRAVE!

This is where **Bravery Missions** come in. A Bravery Mission is when you intentionally put yourself in situations (in small or big ways) so you can learn to face your fears. Each of these missions are a step that will get you closer and closer to your goal and to a mindset where you know that you can totally handle the situation. The more you practice bravery missions, the easier it becomes to do these activities—that process is called **Habituation**.

Habituation happens when you get used to doing something from practicing it over and over. When you do something that scares you over and over again (by facing your fears), your brain and body learn to get used to and even bored by it, and you're no longer scared. You've experienced habituation a lot throughout your life. Remember the first time you sat on a bike? I bet your heart was racing, you put your feet on the pedals and thought, *There's no way I can ride this thing! There's no way I won't fall over!* The more you practiced, the easier it got to sit on the bike, put your feet on the pedals, and go! This is how habituation works. You did it over and over again, and now you don't think twice before grabbing your bike to go for a ride on a nice day. Remember Think + Feel + Do? This is another example of that! With practice, your thoughts changed to, *I got this! I know it gets easier with time* (**Think**), you feel confident in the skills you built by practicing (**Feel**), and now you're able to ride your bike when you want (**Do**).

You can face your fears by practicing Bravery Missions. You decide what is making you feel scared—maybe it's attending soccer tryouts coming up or raising your hand in class—and you then practice small acts of bravery that will get you closer step-by-step to that goal in order to build your bravery skills. Here's a cool and easy-to-do Bravery Mission strategy you can use to be and feel BRAVE. It is called a **Bravery Ladder**.

A Bravery Ladder is a great way to make a step-by-step plan to work on things that make you feel scared or stressed out. It's a crucial part of completing your Bravery Missions, because it helps you gradually practice facing your fears. The idea is to come up with things that you can do that will help you reach your goal. Taking it one step at a time, you gradually challenge yourself to face situations that you've previously avoided.

SEEMS STRAIGHT FORWARD, HUH? LET'S LOOK AT HOW ROWAN TOOK ON THEIR BRAVERY MISSIONS.

Rowan wants to make new friends but feels uncomfortable and shy around new people. They made the choice to face this fear and create a bravery ladder with all the steps necessary to help them accomplish this goal. Rowan decided that this week they will focus on the first step of their Bravery Ladder with this mission: Make eye contact and say, "hi" to someone they'd like to meet at school. On Monday, they told themself, *I can do this! Today I'm going to complete my first bravery mission.*

In English class, they saw a classmate, Katty, they'd been wanting to meet. They tried to look up at Katty when she walked by their desk, but felt nervous and stopped themselves from greeting her. During lunch, Rowan told Luna that they couldn't complete today's Bravery Mission. Luna reminded Rowan that completing Bravery Missions may take a couple of tries and they can totally do it. Luna offered to practice with Rowan so they felt more comfortable before the next time they tried to do it. And on Tuesday, Rowan rocked it! They said hi to Katty in English class, and she said hi back! Rowan successfully completed the first step on their Bravery Ladder.

Let's talk about timing. Some bravery missions, like Rowan's first one, may take a couple of days (or even longer) to complete, and that's OK! It's helpful to identify when you would like to complete your mission by and make a plan for that. You can practice and prepare for some of your bravery missions ahead of time like Rowan and Luna did. You can also support yourself while completing your Bravery Missions by using a Chill-Out Hack (Go back to Level 4 for Chill-Out Hack options), since those will help you tolerate the natural discomfort of facing your fears.

Remember that the goal is to face your fears, not rush to complete your ladder. Because you want habituation to happen, you may need to complete one Bravery Mission a couple of times before you feel more comfortable. For example, let's say Rowan greeted one classmate and that classmate did *not* say "hi" back. Rowan would have to think of another classmate to try and get to know. They would need to keep trying and the more they practice, the easier making eye contact and saying, "hi" to a new person becomes.

For the next week, Rowan focused on their next Bravery Missions, and one by one they followed their plan until they were able to check off each step on their Bravery Ladder and reach the top.

Here's how Rowan's Bravery Ladder looked:

ROWAN'S BRAVERY MISSIONS

Goal: Hang out with a new friend from school.	1: Easiest 10: Hardest
Make eye contact and say "hi" to someone new.	1
Say "bye" to them after class.	2
Smile at them in the hallway.	3
Ask them a general question like, "When is the project in English due?"	4
Ask what they did over the weekend.	5
Ask about plans for this weekend.	6
Invite them to do something together.	7

GOAL: HANG OUT WITH A NEW FRIEND FROM SCHOOL

STEP 7
INVITE THEM TO DO
SOMETHING TOGETHER

STEP 6
ASK ABOUT PLANS
FOR THIS WEEKEND

STEP 5
ASK WHAT THEY DID
OVER THE WEEKEND

STEP 4
ASK THEM A GENERAL
QUESTION LIKE
"WHEN IS THE ENGLISH
PROJECT DUE?"

STEP 3
SMILE AT THEM IN THE
HALLWAY

STEP 2
SAY "BYE" AFTER CLASS

STEP 1
MAKE EYE CONTACT AND SAY,
"HI"

Now that you have a solid idea of how Bravery Missions work, it's time to build your Bravery Ladder and achieve your personal goals!

QUEST

COMPLETE YOUR OWN BRAVERY PLAN

Now you're ready to create your own Bravery Ladder. Grab a piece of paper and something to write with and complete the steps below. You can also make a note in your phone if you have one, or maybe even write these missions into your school planner as part of your daily schedule. If you want to get really organized, you could even set reminders on your phone or use a sticky note to keep you on track.

1. Think about a fear you want to face and identify your goal. You can start by making a list of things that scare or worry you. For example:

- Make new friends
- Join a new friend group
- Try out for a school team
- Participate in a school play
- Sign up for an extracurricular activity or club
- Hang out with friends after school
- Go to a class party

2. List the Bravery Missions you need to complete to accomplish your goal, just like Rowan did.

3. Rank each step, in order from easiest to hardest. Start by writing a "1" next to the easiest situation on your list, working up from there.

4. Now write out all of the steps it will take to accomplish your goal (putting the easiest one at the bottom of the ladder and working up to the hardest missions at the top).

5. Make a list of Chill-Out Hacks that you can use to complete your missions.

6. Set a goal to complete a certain amount of missions per week to keep you on track. Keep climbing up your ladder by completing each mission until you reach the top. It's OK to take your time and even repeat steps, as long as you keep practicing. Be patient with yourself!

7. Once you reach the top of your ladder, reward yourself, because it's hard to face your fears, and you did it! Congrats!

LEVEL UP

SKILLS LEARNED

 Bravery means doing something, even though you feel scared. You can't be brave without feeling scared.

 Fear is often a sign that you are doing something different than what you're used to, and is also a good indicator that you are about to learn something new or to challenge yourself in order to grow.

 Bravery Missions are gradual exposures to feared situations that help you experience **habituation** and grow your bravery skills over time.

Habituation occurs when you do something that scares you over and over again (by facing your fears and taking small steps towards a goal). With repetition and practice, your brain and body get used to it and become comfortable and bored by the experience, so you're no longer scared. Each time you do it you feel less scared and more comfortable doing it!

 Formula for Bravery

1. Remember, you're the boss of your brain. **Do not let fear make choices for you.**

2. Tolerate feeling scared with the help of **Chill-Out Hacks.**

3. Face your fears in a gradual way using a **Bravery Ladder,** plan when you'll do each step, and complete your missions.

NEXT YOU'LL LEARN ABOUT BUILDING YOUR BRAIN SMARTS. SEE YOU THERE!

USING BRAIN
SMARTS TO CHANGE
BRAIN MISTAKES

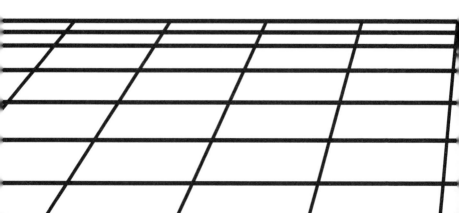

*Y*ou now know that to develop Bravery Skills and become the captain of your own ship, you need to challenge the fear that is trying to take control of your thoughts, feelings, and behaviors.

To keep developing this skill, you also need to build your **Brain Smarts,** which just means your ability to recognize thoughts that are unhelpful and change them to thoughts that are more helpful. In this level you will learn all about how to identify mistakes your brain makes and challenge them, so you will be able to navigate difficult situations and emotions with confidence.

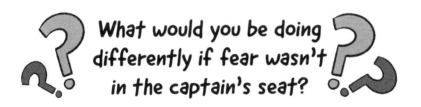

What would you be doing differently if fear wasn't in the captain's seat?

BRAIN MISTAKES (COGNITIVE DISTORTIONS)

Your brain does a great job at so many things! It helps you remember facts for school assignments, communicate with your friends, and even helps your body be coordinated on the field when you play sports or dance at a party. But even though your brain does a great job being in charge of so many things, the fact is that it can make mistakes.

It's true! It's much more common to hear that a person's knee, lungs, or stomach are not working properly or glitching while doing their jobs. Maybe you've had stomach problems like acid reflux, or even need an inhaler to help your lungs work properly if you have asthma. Even though your brain is an organ too, everyone expects this incredibly powerful and helpful organ to be perfect and never make mistakes. But it does! Sometimes brains make mistakes by distorting information and making you believe something that may not be accurate. Here's an example:

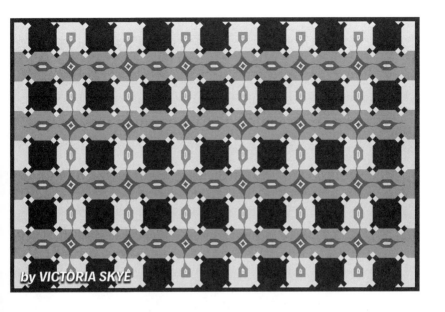

by VICTORIA SKYE

Take a look at this picture. Are the horizontal lines (dark gray lines going left to right) perfectly straight or do they bend?

The horizontal lines appear to bend, but they are actually **completely straight lines.** Your brain is altering the image and making a mistake! But even when your brain makes mistakes like this, there are ways to challenge the error and make sure you are seeing clearly.

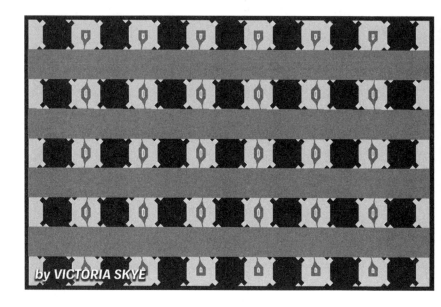

One way we can challenge this brain mistake is to place perfectly straight lines on top of the horizontal lines to see if they fit.

Still not convinced? No problem! That means you need more evidence to catch this Brain Mistake. Let's try one more strategy. **Blur your vision** (squint your eyes) and then see whether the horizontal lines are straight or bend. It might take a second, but if you really squint, the lines should "straighten out"!

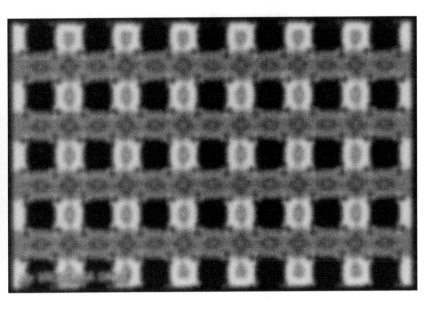

By now, you've collected enough evidence to identify this Brain Mistake and have seen that you can get tricked by things visually, but your brain can twist your thoughts as well.

Luna received an F on her most recent history test. She's having a thought that feels very real to her and seems to make sense. Luna is thinking, *I'm a failure. I'll never pass this class.* However, this thought isn't showing Luna's experiences and reality accurately. Her thoughts are being distorted by the big emotions she's currently feeling, which include disappointment, frustration, and fear. The fact is that Luna has done well in history class so far this quarter.

 Is Luna making a Brain Mistake?

Let's review the **EVIDENCE.** Her past grades in history class are as follows:

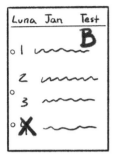
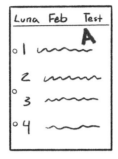
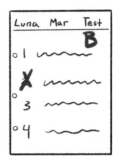

Do you think these are the grades of a student who is failing a class? Me neither! However, Luna really felt like a failure when she received her latest grade because she's experiencing a brain mistake.

BRAIN MISTAKE ALERT! A big clue that you're experiencing a Brain Mistake is when you think how you feel is showing you how things really are, even though there is evidence that contradicts the thought(s).

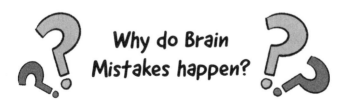

Why do Brain Mistakes happen?

Your brain takes shortcuts sometimes to process all the information it receives. Think about it: you gather so much knowledge on a daily basis (school lessons, conversations with family and friends, media, games, literally everything you see and hear) that your brain has to come up with a system to process all this information and make sense of it all. Every new experience that you have makes neural connections in your brain. Neural connections are like cognitive roads that your thoughts can use over and over once they are created by repetition and practice. More on that in Level 8!

Those connections become your go-to thinking patterns. Because your brain remembers things from the past, it will often take that same road (or neural pathway) when similar thoughts or emotions occur now. This is a good strategy for helping you remember things and process a lot of information, but can be unhelpful when negative thoughts and big emotions are involved. It's important to recognize that your brain is on autopilot when you experience brain mistakes, and that's why they occur without you realizing it. Your brain mistakes show up as automatic thoughts, which is why it can be hard to see them as inaccurate or illogical. Remember that brain mistakes occur because your emotions cloud your judgment, and this makes it hard to see things clearly. Just like what happened to Luna with that history test.

BRAIN MISTAKES ARE THOUGHT PATTERNS THAT ARE IRRATIONAL AND EXAGGERATED BY NEGATIVE THINKING AND FEELINGS. Brain Mistakes are tricky because they convince your mind that what you're thinking is true, even when there is evidence that says otherwise.

REMEMBER, BRAIN MISTAKES:

- Are false, inaccurate, and often exaggerated thoughts that we all experience sometimes.
- Can be caused by strong emotions that cloud your judgement.
- Cause negative emotions.
- May increase stress and negative feelings if not challenged.

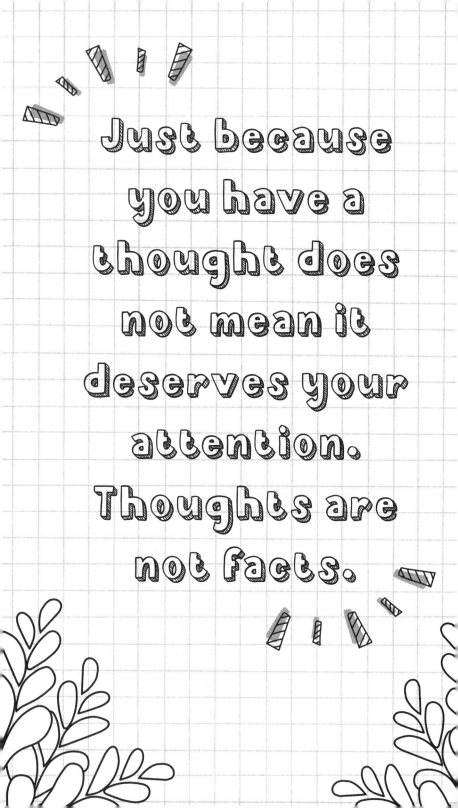

ALL KINDS OF BRAIN MISTAKES

Now you know what Brain Mistakes are and why they show up. Next, you'll learn how to identify them in order to challenge them. Let's get more familiar with these Brain Mistakes.

MIND READING. Your brain uses visual clues to understand how people are feeling and guess what they are thinking all the time. Like if you tell your friend a joke and they laugh, you can assume they thought it was funny without them having to tell you directly. While it is helpful at times to guess what people are thinking, sometimes we just get it wrong. Believing that you know exactly what other people are thinking (and assuming that what they are thinking about you is negative) is a Brain Mistake called **Mind Reading**. A lot of times Mind Reading involves **Projection**, which is when you apply (or project) your own internal worries or feelings onto someone else, making it seem like it's the way *they* are feeling (even though it's actually how *you* are feeling). So, for example, if you are feeling insecure about something, you may project those same thoughts and emotions onto others, even though you really don't know what they are actually thinking or feeling. You assume they are feeling insecure (even though it is you who is feeling insecure). In fact, this happened to Luna last week. Luna waved at Rowan while walking to class and Rowan did not wave back at her. Luna thought, *Rowan's mad at me!* Luna has been feeling insecure in her friendships lately and she projected this insecurity by assuming that Rowan was thinking, *I'm mad at Luna.*

Hey, Otto, wait for me!

When you figure out that you are **Mind Reading** like Luna, you can challenge this kind of Brain Mistake by asking yourself the following:

1. Do I have **proof** this is what they are thinking?

2. What are some **other possible explanations**?

3. **Am I projecting** my insecurities onto them?

Luna challenged this Mind Reading Brain Mistake by answering the challenge questions. She came up with the following **Balanced Thought**:

1. Do I have proof this is what they are thinking? *I don't know that Rowan's mad at me. We hung out yesterday and everything was OK.*

2. What are some other possible explanations? *They might just have their mind on other things, like the test they have after lunch, or maybe they didn't see me when I waved.*

3. Am I projecting my insecurities on to them? *I've been feeling insecure lately about my friendships. I'm projecting my emotions right now.*

FORTUNE-TELLING. Have you ever assumed something would have a negative outcome without considering the actual chance it could be true? Predicting the future sounds like an awesome superpower to have, but unfortunately your brain cannot predict what will happen. But sometimes your brain tricks you into thinking it can! That kind of Brain Mistake is called **Fortune Telling.** Whenever you engage in Fortune-Telling, you expect that negative things will happen and that things will turn out badly. Consider this thought: *I know I will fail the English test this week.*

Has a thought like that crossed your mind before? How do you know for sure that you will fail the test? You likely don't have any proof, but rather, your brain is making a mistake and fortune-telling (predicting the future). If this happens, instead try to challenge Fortune-Telling thoughts like this:

1. Identify your **Prediction**. Describe what you think will happen, when and where it will happen. *What do you think your grade will be?*

2. Rate how likely you think it is that this prediction will actually happen by giving it a score from 0 to 100%.

3. Come up with **evidence for** your Fortune-Telling thought. For example, the evidence for this prediction may be:
    - ☐ I missed a couple of classes when I was out sick
    - ☐ I didn't do all the homework this quarter
    - ☐ I feel anxious

4. Next, think of the **evidence against** this prediction:

- ☐ I passed all the other exams for this class

- ☐ I know a lot of the material because I've been paying attention in class

- ☐ I still have time to prepare for this test

5. Now come up with a **Balanced Thought** using all the **Evidence** you collected, which might sound something like this: *I'm feeling nervous about the test, but I've done well on past tests, understand the material, and have time to prepare. So the chances that I will fail are low.*

ALL–OR–NOTHING THINKING. When you look at things in absolutes or black-and-white categories, that's the **Brain Mistake** called **All-or-Nothing thinking**. All-or-Nothing thinking often involves using extreme expectations in your thinking. You're tipped off to this type of Brain Mistake when your thought includes words like, **Perfect, Always,** or **Never.** This Brain Mistake can make it difficult to see the alternatives in a situation or identify solutions to a problem because you think those extremes are for sure the only outcomes. For example, Rowan had this

All-or-Nothing thought: *If I don't get a perfect 100% on my English project, I'm a failure.*

Rowan can challenge this All-or-Nothing Brain Mistake by changing the absolute terms in their thought to more accurate language using more accurate terms instead.

CHANGE ABSOLUTE TERMS...	TO MORE ACCURATE WORDS ...
Always	Sometimes Often Some Right now
Never	Rarely
Impossible	Difficult Possible with a different approach Maybe Perhaps
Ruined	Needs to be improved/fixed Requires more work or effort
Perfect	Good Good enough Required effort

As with other Brain Mistakes, when you (or Rowan!) are experiencing All-or-Nothing thinking, challenge the thoughts like this:

1. Look for **Evidence** for and against the thought. Think about times when thoughts like this were incorrect. *Getting a grade that is not a 100% does not mean that I am a failure. Failure means that I fail the class. It's okay to have a grade that is good enough and not perfect.*

2. Now come up with a **Balanced Thought** using the evidence you collected. *Even if I don't get a perfect score, I tried my best on this project, learned a lot, and will probably do well.*

MENTAL FILTER. Do you ever just focus on what could go wrong or think everything is just awful because of one little thing that didn't go your way? That's the **Brain Mistake** called **Mental Filter** that occurs when your brain only focuses on the negatives and ignores the positives or the other sides of a situation. For example, Otto woke up this morning and his dad made him his favorite breakfast, pancakes with blueberries. During his first class his teacher let the class watch a movie and brought snacks for everyone. During lunch, the cafeteria ran out of pizza right before it was his turn. Then, during his last class, the teacher gave a pop quiz that he was not prepared for. Otto arrived home and told his dad, *"Today was the worst! Nothing went my way. First no pizza and then a pop quiz I'm sure I failed."*

When you look back on Otto's day, it seems he forgot to consider the good things that happened. Otto could change his thinking and challenge this Mental Filter Brain Mistake like this:

1. Identify the good **and** bad things that occurred.

- **Good things** that happened today:
    - ☐ I had my favorite breakfast
    - ☐ Watched a movie and had snacks during first period
- **Bad things** that happened today:
    - ☐ Cafeteria ran out of pizza
    - ☐ I had a pop quiz that I wasn't ready for

2. Now Otto can come up with a **Balanced Thought** using the Evidence he collected. *Some bad things happened today, but so did some good things that I enjoyed. Today wasn't all bad.*

CATASTROPHIZING. Ever heard of the expression, making mountains out of mole hills? That is an example of a **Brain Mistake** called **Catastrophizing** where your brain jumps to the worst-case scenario and you feel like you can't handle it. It might start with a little worry or concern, and then it snowballs from there, into a much bigger worry. Often, this Brain Mistake starts with *What if...* For example, Rowan didn't do well on their math test. They keep thinking, *What if I don't pass the class? What if I fail and have to repeat the year? Then I won't get to go to high school. What if I don't get into college? Then I won't be able to get a good job and I'll be a failure forever.* Ahh!! Notice how Rowan's first thought snowballed?

ROWAN COULD CHALLENGE THESE CATASTROPHIZING THOUGHTS LIKE THIS:

1. Change the wording of the thought to **be more realistic** about the odds of something happening (you can use the chart from All-or-Nothing thinking to help you with this step).

2. Recognize that you can cope when bad things do happen.

   - Think about what you might need to support yourself during or after this situation if it were to come true.

   - Get some extra support and talk to people that can help you through thinking about this stressful situation.

3. Remind yourself that worrying will make you less able to handle the situation.

4. Come up with a Balanced Thought using all the evidence and support you collected.

Here's what Rowan came up with: *I'm disappointed that I didn't do well on this test. But it's unlikely that*

I'll fail the class, because I've done well on past tests and assignments, and I will plan to be more prepared for the next test coming up. I can handle this situation by asking my teacher for help and reviewing with my parents or friends. I will remember that I've been able to do well in this class before, and with effort I will improve. I'll also listen to my favorite music on the way home today to help me relax and feel confident with this plan. I'll do some Chill-Out Hacks to calm myself down, too. I will also remind myself that worrying won't help me prepare for the next test, but studying will!

EMOTIONAL REASONING. Have you ever been at school and all of a sudden *feel* off or nervous (butterflies in your stomach or your heart feels like it's racing) and because you feel that way, you think something bad might happen? When you use your emotions as proof, instead of using facts, you are experiencing **Emotional Reasoning**. This type of Brain Mistake makes you believe that things are true because they *feel* true. Once, when Otto woke up late, he forgot to eat breakfast because he was rushing and a little worried about a group project he had to present during his second period. He thought to himself, "*I know something really bad is going to happen to me today.*" Otto (and you!) can challenge Emotional Reasoning thinking, by doing the following:

1. Identify what emotion you are experiencing and name it.

2. Come up with some reasons *why* you may be feeling this way.

3. Collect any Evidence you can about why your thought might be true or not true.

4. Now, come up with a Balanced Thought using the Evidence you collected.

Here's what Otto came up with to challenge his Emotional Reasoning: *I may be feeling anxious because I didn't get much sleep last night and also forgot to eat breakfast. I have a group project to present during second period and I always worry when I have to present in front of the class. Nothing bad is going to happen. I need to get a snack and review my notes to feel better about presenting today. Tonight, I'll try to get to bed on time.*

SHOULD–ING. This type of **Brain Mistake** is so common you *should* know what it is! Haha—just kidding. **Should-ing** is simply when you think in rules, like when you have certain expectations about what you and others should or should not do. This Brain Mistake makes you feel guilty or ashamed because when you don't do what you told yourself you should have done, you feel bad about yourself. Similarly, when others don't do what you think they should've done, you feel upset with them. For example, Rowan wants to audition for the school play and has been telling themself that they *should* practice their lines for two hours a day to prepare. Days pass without practicing their lines and Rowan is feeling disappointed and ashamed of themself because they don't feel prepared. How can Rowan challenge this **Should-ing** thought?

1. Reword the thought to remove the word "should" or "shouldn't."

2. Explain the reason and find the evidence for *why* something is a priority or desirable (or not a priority or undesirable to you), without shaming yourself.

3. Come up with a **Balanced Thought** using all the Evidence you collected.

This is what Rowan came up with: *It would be good for me to memorize my lines before the audition. I'll feel more prepared and more confident when I practice ahead of time. I want to be prepared because I'd like to get a good role in the play this year. I'll make some time after dinner to go over my lines, but there's no rule that says I need to practice every day for two hours. Even if I just practice a little bit, I will feel more prepared.*

LABELING. When you do this type of Brain Mistake you are simply calling yourself a name or describing yourself (or someone else) in an unfair way based on a single event or behavior. For example, have you ever thought something like this: *I woke up super late and haven't done anything today.* **I'm so lazy!** Or maybe labeled others, like: *Jake cut in line in front of me today. He's so rude!* **What a jerk.**

Instead, try to challenge this type of Brain Mistake by:

1. Change the wording to label the event, not the person.

- Instead of labeling yourself, **describe what you did**.

- Instead of labeling others, **describe what they did.**

2. Come up with a **Balanced Thought** using the wording that describes the event, not the person.

- *Today I got up later than expected and loafed around the house because I was feeling tired. I can enjoy some downtime now, and later I'll work on my science project.*

- *Jake cut in line in front of me at the cafeteria today. That was kind of a rude thing to do, but he's a good friend and is usually thoughtful and respectful. Maybe he was rushing because he had somewhere to be.*

BLAMING. Blaming yourself for things that are not in your control or blaming others for things not in their control is another type of **Brain Mistake.** Sound familiar? You blame yourself for something you weren't entirely responsible for, or you blame other people and overlook ways you may have contributed to the problem. For example, you might think to yourself: *I didn't make a goal during the soccer game today. It's all my fault we lost!* Or you might **blame others**: *It's not my fault that I failed the test, because the teacher made the questions way too hard, and I was distracted by my classmate tapping a pencil on the desk during the exam.*

To challenge these Blaming thoughts ask yourself:

- What factors are **in your control?**
- What factor are **out of your control?**

Come up with a Balanced Thought considering what was and was not in your control or the other person's control.

1. *I didn't make a goal today, but another teammate missed a goal too, we were already behind by two goals and the other team has had more practices.*

2. *I wasn't as prepared as I would have liked for today's test because the questions were hard. I can ask my teacher for help preparing for the next exam, and in the future, I can ask to be moved to a different seat if I'm feeling distracted during a test.*

Sometimes, it's best to eliminate **Blaming** all together, because you won't always be able to identify who or what to blame in a situation. So, an additional way to challenge this **Brain Mistake** is to be a **Neutral Observer.** This means to describe the situation without personal attachment, and problem-solve from there. Take a neutral look at the situation by describing it and then identify what needs to be done to fix it without blaming.

So, consider this: You left a book you need to finish your homework at school. You could blame yourself and get mad and frustrated. Instead try thinking like a **Neutral Observer** like this: *I left my book at school, that can happen to anyone. I can ask to go back to school to get it or get to school early tomorrow to finish my homework.*

Looking for more ways to challenge brain mistakes? Here are more strategies:

ADVICE FOR A FRIEND

This is a great strategy that you can use whenever you think you're experiencing a Brain Mistake. When you're talking to a friend, you are more likely to be rational, forgiving, and encouraging. So think about what you would say to a friend who comes to you for advice with the very same thought you're having. It's much easier to recognize when someone else is thinking irrationally, so a great way to challenge your own brain mistakes is to pretend that you are talking to a friend and giving them some good advice.

Think about the following:

- Can you recognize anything that sounds exaggerated or inaccurate in the thought?

- Would you be harsh or kind with your friend to help them with this thought?

- What advice would you give them?

Then, give yourself the same advice you'd give a friend. This is a great mental hack and helps you think clearly and catch pesky brain mistakes effectively.

MORE BRAIN MISTAKE BUSTERS

Here are more questions you can ask yourself when identifying and challenging your brain mistakes.

- What is a more helpful thought?

- What is another way of looking at this situation?

- What would people who care about me say to me in this situation?

- What is the worst that could really happen?

- Can I be 100% sure that this is true?

- If the worst really did happen, what could I do to deal with it, and who could help me?

- What is the best possible outcome of this situation?

Additionally, to catch and challenge Brain Mistakes you can...

IDENTIFY IT/NOTICE IT: The first step is simply to become aware of unhelpful thoughts & thinking styles. Notice it & name it.

CHALLENGE IT: Not all thoughts are true. Time to check out if it's realistic & to gently challenge it. Some useful questions to ask yourself: **WHAT WOULD I SAY TO MY BEST FRIEND IF THEY HAD THIS THOUGHT? DO I HAVE PROOF FOR THIS THOUGHT?**

RE-WRITE IT: Come up with a more realistic, kind, helpful, healthy, & balanced thought.

BE MINDFUL: You can also just simply observe the thought, without judgment, & allow it to pass.

DISTRACT: Or you can try distracting yourself from unhelpful or repetitive thoughts with healthy activities.

Level 6
Final Quest
BRAIN MISTAKE LOG

Now it's time for you to identify and challenge your own brain mistakes. Grab a piece of paper and something to write with. Create a template like this one. Think about a time this week when you may have experienced a brain mistake, and fill out each column by answering the prompts provided. Remember, you can review how to challenge each brain mistake by going back to pages 153–173. You got this!

MY BRAIN MISTAKE LOG

SITUATION	THOUGHT(S)	NAME THE BRAIN MISTAKE	CHALLENGE	MY BALANCED THOUGHT(S)
Describe the situation.	Include the automatic thought(s) you had that could be a Brain Mistake. *What was I thinking when this happened?*	What kind of Brain Mistake is this? Mind Reading Fortune Telling All-or-nothing Thinking Mental Filter Catastrophizing Emotional Reasoning Should-ing Labeling Blaming	Challenge the Brain Mistake depending on which one is showing up for you here. You can review how to challenge Brain Mistakes on pages 153–173.	Create a Balanced Thought(s) using all the Evidence you collected in the "Challenge" column.

LEVEL UP

SKILLS LEARNED

 Your brain is not perfect and makes mistakes, **Brain Mistakes**. Your brain makes mistakes by altering information and making you see or believe something that **may not be accurate**.

 Brain Mistakes are thought patterns that are irrational and exaggerated by negative thinking and feelings. Brain mistakes are tricky because they convince your mind that what you're thinking is true, even when you have evidence otherwise. Brain mistakes occur automatically in your normal day-to-day thoughts. This sometimes makes them difficult to recognize and challenge.

Brain mistakes discussed in this level are:

- Mind Reading
- Fortune telling
- All-or-nothing thinking
- Mental Filter
- Catastrophizing

- Emotional Reasoning
- Should-ing
- Labeling
- Blaming

 Challenge each **Brain Mistake** by asking questions that will support finding the **Evidence** needed to think clearly and create a more **Balanced Thought.**

 A good way to challenge a **Brain Mistake** is to think, *What advice would I give to a friend who had the same thought?*

 You can always use a **Brain Mistake log** to identify and challenge brain mistakes when they come up.

Great job leveling up your **Brain Smarts**. You're well on your way to having all the tools you need to manage stress, big emotions, and glitchy thinking in effective ways. Next, we'll discuss how to build your **Emotion Smarts**. See you there!

LEVEL 7

EMOTIONAL INTELLIGENCE: BUILDING YOUR EMOTION SMARTS

E motions play an important role in your life. Studies show that people with a good understanding of their emotions are better at communicating with others, managing their stress, resolving conflicts, having positive relationships, and effectively overcoming life challenges. Emotions are part of your everyday life. Since waking up this morning you've experienced a couple of different emotions already. Perhaps you felt *anticipation* for the school day, or maybe you felt *nervous* for a quiz you had coming up. Emotions accompany you throughout your life, so it's beneficial for you to learn more about them to know what to do when they show up.

But emotions are tricky sometimes, aren't they? They can show up out of the blue and sometimes you're left feeling confused about what you are experiencing or what to do about it. This is why I want to equip you with all the tools you need to understand and manage your emotions better. Some people call understanding your emotions and your ability to regulate how you feel Emotional

Intelligence but I like to call it your **Emotion Smarts**.

EMOTIONAL INTELLIGENCE (OR EMOTION SMARTS) IS THE ABILITY TO UNDERSTAND, IDENTIFY, USE, SHARE, AND MANAGE YOUR EMOTIONS IN AN EFFECTIVE AND POSITIVE WAY.

To get your Emotion Smarts leveled-up, first you need to understand that there are six basic human emotional states:

1. **Sadness:** emotional state that occurs when feeling disappointment, loss, or hopelessness.

2. **Happiness:** a pleasant emotional state that produces feelings of joy, contentment, and satisfaction.

3. **Fear:** an emotion that is important for survival and triggers your fight, flight, freeze, or fawn responses.

4. **Anger:** an emotional state leading to feelings of aggression, irritability, and frustration.

5. **Surprise:** a brief emotional response, either positive or negative, that happens when something unexpected occurs.

6. **Disgust:** a strong emotion that results in feeling repulsed by a person, situation, or thing.

These six emotional states are at the core of what you might be feeling and form the basis of a range of emotions. Still it can be difficult to identify exactly what emotion you are feeling sometimes. That's where Feelings Charts and the **Body Clues Emotions Chart** come in handy. These are easy to use, all you have to do is match the way you feel to the descriptions or words on the chart and work your way back towards the center to figure out the exact emotion you are feeling. Smart, huh?

A GREAT WAY TO GET TO KNOW YOUR EMOTIONS BETTER IS BY LOOKING TO YOUR BODY CLUES, OR YOUR PHYSICAL RESPONSE TO A SITUATION. YOUR BODY IS YOUR GUIDE!

BODY CLUES EMOTIONS CHART

The **Body Clues Emotions Chart** is a great tool to help you label emotions by first identifying how your body is responding, then figuring out what feeling you're experiencing.

You'll notice that the Chart has four columns. The first column is where you can find descriptions of **where** you feel an increase or decrease in energy or sensation in your body. Have you ever noticed that when you're sad you may feel tired and prefer to stay home instead of going out with friends? This is because when you are sad, you have less energy in your arms and legs, making you feel tired.

The second column is where you can find descriptions of the **behaviors** that may come with emotions such as *crying* and *tiredness* (both body clues for **Sadness**).

The third column includes secondary emotions. Secondary emotions are emotional reactions you have to other emotions. For example, you may feel *disappointed* that your friends went out to the movies without you.

This leads us to the last column where you'll find the basic or primary emotion. You are feeling sad.

BODY CLUES EMOTIONS CHART

WHERE I FEEL THE EMOTION	BEHAVIORS I AM NOTICING	SECONDARY EMOTION	CORE EMOTION
Increased sensation in your chest and head; decreased energy in your legs	• Jumpy • Sweaty Palms • Breathless • Speechless • Eyebrows Up • Fluttery • Tingly Sensation • Jaw Drop	• Shocked • Confused • Delighted • Excited	**SURPRISE**
Increased sensation in your entire body	• Smiling • Speaking in an upbeat tone of voice • Standing tall • Calm • Relaxed • Warm • Butterflies in your stomach • Buzzing	• Peaceful • Amused • Proud • Optimistic	**HAPPY**
Increased sensation in your chest and head; decreased activation in your arms, legs, and feet	• Frowning • Looking down • Slouching • Crying • Being quiet • Wanting to be alone • Feeling tired • Slow heart rate	• Lonely • Abandoned • Disappointed • Guilty	**SAD**
Increased sensation in your chest and head, excluding your arms and some activation in your feet	• Fast heartbeat • Racing thoughts • Overthinking/overplanning • Tense • Avoiding people, places, and things • Feeling a pit or knot in your stomach • Feeling frozen in place • Fidgety	• Embarrassed or unwanted • Inferior • Insecure • Scared	**FEAR**
Increased sensation in your belly, mouth, and forehead area	• Need to move • Scrunched face • Nausea • Lump in throat • Feeling queasy • Turning away • Shuddering	• Dislike • Offended • Disapproval • Aversion/avoidance	**DISGUST**
Increased sensation in upper half of your body and arms	• Frowning • Loud words • Heart racing • Clenched jaw • Gut-turning • Unsafe behaviors (throwing, hitting, etc.) • Feeling hot	• Hurt • Mad • Aggressive • Annoyed	**ANGER**

HOW TO USE THE BODY CLUES EMOTIONS CHART

1. Start on the first column of the chart and identify where in your body you feel an **increase or decrease in energy.**

2. Then move towards the second column of the chart to identify the **behaviors** that you are engaging in. Sometimes you experience a couple of behaviors next to your identified energy zone. That's OK—all behaviors in that same section can be considered.

3. Then move towards the third column in the chart to identify the **secondary emotion**. Sometimes, the secondary emotion you're experiencing is not exactly right next to the behavior you've identified. That's OK—the secondary emotions in the same section can all be considered.

4. Once you've identified the secondary emotion, move on to the last column to identify the basic emotion you're feeling.

Check out how Luna used the Body Clues Emotions Chart when she was struggling:

"I woke up for school one day and noticed that I had all this energy in my head and chest but also I could feel it throughout my *entire body!* Then, I looked at the second column and found *smiling* and *buzzing.* In the third column, I found the secondary emotion I was feeling: *optimistic!* All of these were in the **happy** section of the chart. That made sense since I was really looking forward to seeing the new otter exhibit with my friends."

EMOTION CHARTS

Another great way to figure out how you are feeling is by using an **Emotion Chart.** The chart includes the name of the emotion as well as how it's expressed (which is another way of saying how that emotion looks or shows up in your body or on your face). Go ahead and identify how you're feeling right now using the chart on the next page.

TODAY I FEEL...

NOW THAT YOU ARE WELL ON YOUR WAY TO UNDERSTANDING WHAT YOU ARE FEELING, THE NEXT STEP IS TO COMMUNICATE YOUR EMOTIONS LIKE A BOSS! Emotion Smarts require you to not only know *what emotion* you're experiencing, but also know *how to share and express your emotions* effectively with others. What are some effective ways to share emotions with others?

Keep in mind that it's important to teach others how to treat you. We're all different because we perceive the world in different ways based on your experiences, thoughts, background, etc. Therefore, you cannot predict what others think or need, and others cannot know what you need if you don't communicate your needs. An important part of developing your Emotion Smarts is that you not only know *what* you are feeling, but that you also know *how* to explain and share your emotions and needs with others in a non-reactive way.

Let's learn two communication strategies that will help you communicate with others effectively: **I-Statements** and **Offer & Seek Validation**.

I-Statements are an effective communication strategy that helps you communicate emotions to others confidently and respectfully. This strategy helps you clearly communicate how you are feeling, what is making you feel that way, and what you need from the other person.

I-STATEMENT FORMULA

I-statement formula for effective communication:

You:

I feel _____ (emotion) **when you**

_____ (describe behavior)

because _____ (reason). *I would prefer that you*

_____ (offer a solution)

so that _____ (clarify solution).

Listener:

What I heard you say is _____

(summarize what communicator shared).

Did I get that right?

You:

Yes or offer a correction.

Let's practice using the I-Statement formula with Rowan's help.

During lunch their friend Sophie came up to them and asked them to give her their math homework to copy because she didn't have time to finish it last night. Rowan felt confused and wasn't sure how to respond. They were feeling scared that they would get in trouble for sharing the homework. They didn't want to be mean to Sophie, but also didn't want to share their work. They felt so nervous about the consequences of getting caught! Then Rowan remembered that they could use the **I-Statement Formula** and look at the **Body Clues Emotions Chart** to help out.

This is what Rowan came up with:

Hey Sophie, I felt nervous when you asked me to share my homework with you because we could both get in trouble with Mr. Green for sharing answers. I would prefer that you finish the homework on your own or I can help you with it so that neither of us get accused of cheating.

ANOTHER STRATEGY FOR EFFECTIVE COMMUNICATION IS CALLED OFFER & SEEK VALIDATION: When you use validating language, you communicate to others that their feelings make sense and that you understand where they're coming from, without judgment. When you validate others, they feel heard and understood by you, and when others feel understood by you, they are better able to understand you back. Win-win! This strategy offers a collaborative communication technique that helps people feel heard, supports addressing each other's needs effectively, and as a bonus can make your relationships stronger.

To offer **Validation** to others, make sure to communicate that you understand what the other person is feeling or experiencing and that it makes sense to you. For example, your dad asked you to put away your shoes from the front door after school, you forgot to put them away and the next day he tripped over your shoes and bumped his knee.

STEPS TO VALIDATING OTHERS:

1. **Identify what happened.** *My dad asked me to put away my shoes, I forgot, and then he tripped on them the next day.*

2. **Why is the other person feeling this way? Is there a good reason?** *My dad is upset because he asked me to do something, and I didn't do it. My dad is also upset because he asked me to put my shoes away to avoid someone tripping over them.*

3. **Is there something you did or did not do to contribute to them feeling this way? (Taking responsibility)** *I did not put away my shoes. It was my responsibility to put them away when I was asked, and I forgot. Because I forgot to put the shoes away, my dad tripped on them.*

4. **Explain to the other person exactly why you understand what they are feeling and offer a solution for next time.**

VALIDATING LANGUAGE IN THIS SITUATION COULD SOUND LIKE: *Dad, I'm sorry I forgot to put away my shoes when you asked me to. I realize that you asked me to put them away because they're in the way and someone could get hurt, and then you got hurt. I'm sorry, I should have put them away. I'll make sure to do what you ask right away next time.*

Dad's response: *Thank you for apologizing and taking responsibility. We all forget to do what we're told sometimes. I appreciate you making sure to keep the door clear from now on.*

Seeking validation supports your ability to connect with others and help them understand what you need. For example, your mom asks you to start your homework right after getting home from school. You tell her that you're tired and will get started on it later. Dinner time comes around and your mom asks you if you've finished your homework and you tell her that you'll start after dinner. Your mom comes into your room at bedtime and sees you at your desk working on your homework. You let your mom know you need more time to finish an assignment you have due tomorrow. Your mom gets upset and tells you that you should have started working on it earlier and now you'll be up late and won't get enough sleep.

STEPS to seeking validation from others:

1. **Identify what you need in this situation.**
   I need my mom to understand that I had a really hard football practice after school, I was so tired and needed to chill before dinner. I also need my mom to know that I'm not sure how to complete this assignment because I left the book I need in my locker.

2. **Why is the other person feeling this way? Is there a good reason?** *My mom wanted me to start my homework early so I would get to bed on time. She knows that when I'm tired I have a hard time getting ready in the morning and focusing in class.*

3. **Is there something you did or did not do to contribute to them feeling this way? (Taking responsibility)** *I didn't start my homework when she asked me to, and I also didn't explain why I was delaying.*

4. **Explain to the other person exactly why you understand what they are feeling and offer a solution for next time.**

SEEKING VALIDATION LANGUAGE IN THIS SITUATION COULD SOUND LIKE: *Mom, I understand why you asked me to start my homework early. I've been going to bed late and when I don't get enough sleep, the next day can be hard for me because I'm tired. I didn't start my homework right away because I was spent after practice, and I also forgot one of the books I need to finish an assignment at school. I tried to search for the information online but couldn't find what I needed. Would you take me to school*

early tomorrow so I can grab my book and finish that
assignment during first period?

Mom's response: *I understand being tired after a*
long day. Thanks for letting me know what was going
on. Next time, let me know right away and we can
go get your book or help you make a plan to get the
assignment done.

Let's see how Otto uses the **Offer & Seek
Validation** skill...

Otto's parents asked him to take out the trash last
night to make sure that their dog, Ziggy, didn't get
into it while everyone was at work and school the
next day. Otto forgot to take out the trash. When he
got home from school his mom was upset that Ziggy
had ripped the trash bag open and there was garbage
all over the kitchen floor. Otto knew he messed up
and didn't know how to explain to his mom why he
forgot. Otto knew he should acknowledge why his
mom was upset (offer validation) and also explain
(seek validation) why he had forgotten to do what
she asked.

Otto came up with the following:

Mom, I'm really sorry I forgot to take out the trash last night. I know that my forgetting to do what you asked caused a mess in our kitchen, and that Ziggy could have gotten sick from getting into the garbage. I forgot to take out the trash because I stayed up late reviewing my health project and fell asleep before getting it done. I will make sure to set a reminder on my phone or take out the trash right away next time, so this doesn't happen again. Can I help you clean up?

 **But what about when you're just too overwhelmed to use any strategies?**

When this happens, a great strategy to use is **HALT**. This acronym reminds you to check in on basic things you need in order to be able to think clearly and support yourself.

HALT stands for:

Am I HUNGRY?

Am I ANGRY?

Am I LONELY?

Am I TIRED?

So, when it all feels like way too much, check in with **HALT** and make sure to address these needs before figuring out which chill-out hack you can use next. For example, if you are tired, hold off on making any decisions and support yourself by getting to bed early.

Quest

EMOTION SMARTS MISSION

Read the scenario below and try to identify the body clues (physical responses), emotion(s), and best way to respond to the problem described. You can use the Body Clues Emotions Chart or Feelings Chart to figure out how Luna is feeling.

- Luna knew that her friend and field hockey teammate Cassidy was planning a sleepover at her house this weekend. Luna found out that some of her friends had already heard from Cassidy about the sleepover details and she had not heard from her just yet. She made sure to check her texts, and nothing. Luna saw Cassidy in the hallway at school and felt shaky, her heart started beating really fast, and her cheeks felt hot. Luna wasn't sure she would get invited to the sleepover and wondered if Cassidy was mad at her, or she had done something wrong.

Grab a piece of paper and something to write with and help Luna identify the following:

- What are Luna's body clues?
- What behavior(s) emotion(s) do you think Luna is experiencing?
- How should Luna respond?

Here's another one. Read the scenario below and come up with a good **Offer & Seek Validation** for Rowan.

- Rowan's parents are on them about always being on their phone after school, and keep telling them they need to cut back on their screen time. Rowan needs to coordinate with classmates about school projects and this is also the only way they are able to communicate with their friends outside of school.

- How should Rowan respond to their parents' request?

ANSWER KEY:

What are Luna's body clues? She felt shaky, heart racing, cheeks felt hot.

What behavior(s) and emotion(s) do you think Luna is experiencing? She was checking her texts and feeling confused, anxious, and hurt.

How could Luna respond? Wait to be invited to the sleepover or ask Cassidy if everything is OK.

Rowan's offer and seek validation statement: *Mom, Dad, I know you're worried about my time on screens, but this is my main way of talking to classmates and friends outside of school. Can we add time to my screen time so I'm able to coordinate what I need to complete for school assignments and also stay connected with friends?*

Updates: Luna saw Cassidy at field hockey practice that afternoon and asked her if everything was OK. Cassidy let her know she had a really busy day, was rushing to get some homework done before practice, and can't wait for Luna to come over this weekend for the sleepover. Luna had a great time at Cassidy's. Rowan's parents understood and worked with them to add to their screen time in a way that worked for the family.

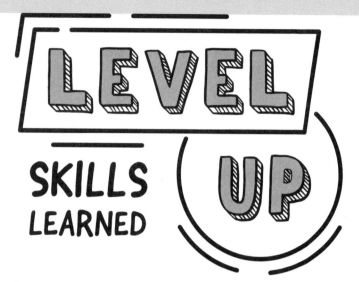

LEVEL UP

SKILLS LEARNED

 Emotional Intelligence or **Emotion Smarts** is the ability to understand, identify, use, share, and manage your emotions in an effective.

 Your primary **Emotions** include:

1. Sadness

2. Happiness

3. Fear

4. Anger

5. Surprise

6. Disgust

You can use the **Body Clues Emotions Chart** and **Feelings Chart** to help you identify emotions effectively.

 Once you identify what you are feeling, you can communicate your needs to others by using **I-Statements, Offer & Seek Validation, and HALT** skills.

CONGRATULATIONS ON COMPLETING LEVEL 7! KEEP GOING AND LEARN ABOUT THE HOW OF HAPPINESS NEXT. SEE YOU THERE!

HOW TO
FEEL GOOD

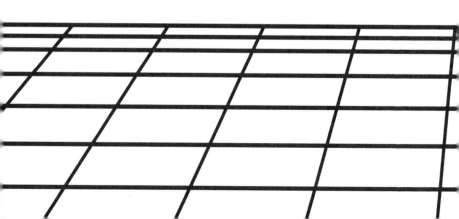

When you feel stressed, do you ever have someone tell you *just be happy* or *I just want you to be happy*? Whenever you're struggling with something, it's hard to hear that you should feel differently, especially if you're feeling stressed, frustrated, or disappointed. In the last level, you learned about your Emotion Smarts and all the feelings you experience as a human being. However, of all your basic emotions, none seems to get more attention than **HAPPINESS.** It makes sense, because we all want to feel happy, but what does that really mean? When people that love you say, *I just want you to be happy* what they really mean may be...

- I want you to **enjoy** your life.
- I want you to **feel good** about yourself.
- I want you to **experience joy** and things you like.
- I want the **best for you**.

Those are wonderful things to strive for, but the reality is that happiness alone will not accomplish all these goals. The truth is that you don't have to feel happy all the time to feel good about your life, enjoy it, and live confidently. Life is like a rollercoaster:

you'll experience really great highs (happy, blissful, and proud moments), neutral moments (time spent working towards your goals or when things are just calm) and then drops and loops that can make your stomach turn (sad, stressful, or angry moments).

Life is the entire rollercoaster ride, start to finish. A rollercoaster with just highs wouldn't make much sense and would actually get boring. The neutral and low moments make those highs special and worth appreciating. You need to experience the whole ride to really enjoy everything the rollercoaster (and life) has to offer.

To understand happiness better, we should first debunk some myths about this emotion.

MYTH #1: HAPPINESS IS THE ONLY EMOTION WORTH FEELING.

FACT #1: When you believe that happiness is the only emotion worth feeling, you may think that all other emotions are bad or useless when they show up. Believing this may make you want to avoid feeling other emotions like sadness, anger, and fear. The truth is **all emotions are important, helpful, and expected.** Every emotion gives you vital information about what you need or need to do in a particular situation. Let's review your basic emotions below.

SADNESS

HAPPINESS

FEAR

ANGER

SURPRISE

DISGUST

MYTH #2: HAPPINESS IS THE ULTIMATE GOAL.

FACT #2: Happiness is an emotion and not a goal or destination. Emotions are temporary, meaning that they come and go. So we can't feel happy and continue to feel that way forever. You've felt sad, mad, stressed, and these feelings didn't last forever, right? That's because **all emotions are temporary**. If happiness is your ultimate goal, and you feel it and then that feeling goes away, you will feel disappointed. Instead, be mindful and grateful when you feel the wonderful effects of happiness, and remind yourself that moments like these will come, and go, and come back around again.

MYTH #3: IF I'M NOT HAPPY ALL THE TIME, THERE'S SOMETHING WRONG WITH ME.

FACT #3: You just learned when we debunked myth #2 that happiness is an emotion and emotions are temporary. The expectation that if you're not happy all the time it means that there is something wrong with you is not accounting for the fact that life is unpleasant at times. The truth is that if you're not happy all the time, you're completely normal! You also know that all emotions have a purpose, and in order to navigate all the ups and downs of life, you will need to experience them all.

HAPPINESS IS NOT THE ULTIMATE GOAL. YOU DON'T HAVE TO FEEL HAPPY ALL THE TIME TO FEEL GOOD, AND ALL EMOTIONS ARE OK.

Happiness is a **feeling of pleasure and positivity.** Happiness is mistakenly thought of as the opposite of sadness, but it's actually more like a combination of things that come together and make you feel good about yourself and your life. Happiness researchers define happiness as "the experience of joy, contentment, or wellness, combined with a sense that your life is good, meaningful, and worthwhile." Psychologists also explain that *feeling satisfied with life circumstances* (friendships, accomplishments, and things that are important to you) and *how good you feel on a daily basis* (feeling light, smiley, or content more often than not) both contribute to your happiness as well.

So, the two key elements of happiness are:

1. Experiencing more positive emotions in your daily life.

2. Feeling satisfied with your life.

HAPPINESS KEY #1: INCREASING POSITIVE EMOTIONS

Positive emotions feel good and they're good for you. It makes sense that happiness is associated with experiencing more positive feelings, because when you feel good, you feel other positive emotions as well, such as gratitude, hope, love, and excitement.

Research shows that when you increase feel-good emotions in your daily life, the benefits are amazing. You will:

- Feel happier and more content.
- Strengthen your immune system, so you get sick less often (bonus!).
- Protect your cardiovascular system, making your heart stronger.
- Improve your performance at school.
- Decrease your levels of stress.
- Focus less on uncomfortable, unwanted, or difficult emotions!

There are a lot of great things that come from being happy, so it's totally understandable why you would want more of it!

HAPPINESS KEY #2: LIFE SATISFACTION (FEELING GOOD ABOUT YOUR LIFE)

Feeling satisfied with your life means liking the way your life is going, in an overall sense. This means that your needs, wishes, and expectations are being met in different areas of your life, including your relationships, friendships, and academic achievements. For example, perhaps getting good grades is important to you, so you study hard and then get a good grade. You may think that getting the good grade is what makes you feel good. That doesn't hurt! But the truth is that it's the effort that you put into your goals that makes you feel satisfied, regardless of the outcome! So the more you identify personal goals, work towards those goals, and learn what works during the process, the more satisfied you will feel with your life. Which leads to the importance of having an **Internal Locus of Control**.

HAVING AN INTERNAL LOCUS OF CONTROL HAS BEEN ASSOCIATED WITH INCREASED HOPE, IMPROVED MOOD, AND BETTER DECISION-MAKING.

Locus of Control refers to how strongly you believe that you have control over what happens in your life. People with an **External Locus of Control** believe that their successes or failures result from external factors (things outside of their control), such as luck, circumstance, or other people's actions. People that have an **Internal Locus of Control** understand that *they* are the ones that have control over the events that influence their lives.

What kind of Locus of Control do you think you have?

I determine my future; I make things happen. Look what I can do!

INTERNAL
Locus of Control

Things happen to me. There is nothing I can do about my future. Why does everything happen to me? Why bother?

EXTERNAL
Locus of Control

Happiness is a powerful positive emotion, but it's not the only one you need to make you feel good. Did you know that feeling good about your life is also a skill that you can build with consistent practice? That's right! **HAPPINESS RESEARCH SHOWS THAT TO FEEL GOOD, IT TAKES EFFORT AND PRACTICE, WHICH IS TOTALLY IN YOUR CONTROL.** This means you have the ability to influence how good you feel in your life. Research shows that by engaging in activities and practices that both increase your positive emotions and feelings of life satisfaction, you are able to feel better and happier. Here are some things that research shows support you feeling good:

FEEL GOOD HACKS

GET MOVING! Regular movement increases the chemicals in your brain (endorphins, dopamine, and adrenaline) that are associated with feeling happy, confident, capable, and less stressed. It is recommended that you engage in physical activity (any kind of movement) for at least 60 minutes each day. You can develop this healthy habit by starting with 20 minutes a day and build up from there.

SPEND TIME IN NATURE! Scientists have discovered that just spending time walking among or simply looking at trees improves your mood, lowers your blood pressure, and reduces the stress-related hormones cortisol and adrenaline. So, get out there! Get outside and go for a nature walk or gaze up at the stars on a clear night.

PRACTICE ACTS OF KINDNESS! Researchers have learned some pretty amazing things studying kindness. When you practice random acts of kindness, your brain's reward center is activated and releases mood-boosting and pain-relieving neurochemicals called dopamine and serotonin. In fact, just witnessing a kind act can release these feel-good chemicals. Volunteering and helping others will also improve your physical and mental wellbeing.

PRACTICE BEING MINDFUL AND PRESENT! Mindfulness has been well studied and definitely helps you be healthier, less affected by stress, be and more relaxed, creative, and open to learning. Mindfulness also helps you sleep better and improves your relationships with others, which also helps you feel happier and more satisfied with your life. Being mindful works! Simple mindfulness practices like we talked about in Level 4 (Chill-Out Hacks) make you feel happier by helping you slow down, appreciate your surroundings, and notice things that make you happy. It's a win-win!

LOOK FOR THE FREE SMILING MIND APP. YOU CAN FIND CUSTOMIZED PROGRAMS THAT WILL HELP YOU PRACTICE BEING MINDFUL EVERY DAY.

LEARN A NEW SKILL! Learning new things exposes you to new ideas and helps you stay curious about and engaged in the world and your life. It also gives you a sense of accomplishment and helps boost self-confidence and resilience. Is there something you've always wanted to learn to do and haven't just yet? Go ahead and give it a try. Checking out clubs or extracurricular activities that you find interesting at school or in your community is also a great way to learn new skills.

FIND AND PLAN SOMETHING FUN! Having something to look forward to, like spending time with a friend or planning a family hangout, makes you feel good and anticipate good things happening in the future, which increases hope. (More on the power of hope later in this Level. Stay tuned!) So, take a minute and think about something you've been wanting to plan with your friends or family. Perhaps it's a surprise party for your friend's birthday that's coming up, or a nearby hiking trail you want to check out, or a family game night you want to plan. You get to choose. Research shows that even just the effort of planning things that you will enjoy in the future makes you feel good!

SET A GOAL FOR YOURSELF! Setting a personal goal and working towards that goal makes you feel good and makes you feel optimistic about the future. When you identify something that you want to achieve for yourself such as improving your grade in a class, joining a club at school this year, or making a new friend, it makes you feel confident and in control of your life. After all, you've made a choice and are working towards a desired outcome. The efforts put towards your new goal will also help you explore new situations and develop skills you didn't have before, which will also make you feel proud and accomplished.

 **WHAT'S A GOAL YOU WOULD LIKE TO WORK TOWARD?**

DO WHAT YOU KNOW! Doing something you enjoy and know you're already good at can make you feel capable and confident, which in turn makes you feel good. Win-win! Maybe you enjoy cooking and trying out new recipes at home. Your family and friends rave about the recipes you come up with, and you love being able to impress them with your delicious new creations. Maybe you're a solid baseball player. You go to practice every week and consistently work on your skills, so when it's game time and you get to do what you do best—play—it feels great!

EXPRESS GRATITUDE! Send a thank you note to someone you appreciate. Research shows that feeling and expressing gratitude helps you have more feel-good emotions, appreciate what's good in your life, and build strong relationships. More on the power of gratitude later in this level.

CONNECT WITH FRIENDS! Friends make you happier! It is scientifically proven that spending time with friends reduces stress and has a positive influence on your mood. In fact, researchers have found that making new friends can lift your spirits through the release of oxytocin (a feel good hormone). So go ahead and plan that sleepover or group outing with your friends.

Mini Quest
HOW TO FEEL GOOD

What are some things that make YOU feel good? Make a list, on paper or in your phone, of things that bring you joy so that you can remember them next time you need a mood boost. Think about your favorite foods, people, places, experiences, music, etc., and include those in your feel-good list!

MORE EMOTIONS THAT HELP YOU FEEL GOOD

There are two special emotions that play a big role in you feeling good. **Gratitude** and **Hope** are emotions that support and increase your overall experience of wellbeing in your life, as well as protect you from feeling overwhelmed by stress when things get tough. Let's check them out.

GRATITUDE IS A FEELING YOU HAVE WHEN YOU ARE THANKFUL AND APPRECIATE SOMETHING YOU RECEIVE. This can be a gift (*tangible* or something you can touch) or someone helping you out (*intangible* or something you're not able to touch, like someone's time and effort to support you). Experiencing and expressing gratitude has many benefits, including improvements in your:

- Relationships and friendships
- Physical health
- Quality of sleep
- Self-esteem

GRATITUDE IS ALL ABOUT FOCUSING ON WHAT'S GOOD IN YOUR LIFE AND BEING THANKFUL FOR THE THINGS YOU HAVE RATHER THAN FOCUSING ON WHAT YOU DON'T HAVE JUST YET. There are ways to boost gratitude that I like to call **Feel-Good Hacks.**

LIST 3 GOOD THINGS. This is a fun and simple exercise guaranteed to increase gratitude and boost your mood. Here's how:

1. Have a notebook or piece of paper and something to write with next to your bed.

2. Every night before you go to bed, think of three good things that happened during the

day. Don't worry about whether they're big or small—anything positive or that you liked that happened that day counts. For example, perhaps you got to talk to a friend during lunch, got test results back and found out you rocked it, or listened to your favorite song on your way to school.

3. Write these 3 things down. Don't skip this! Writing is an important step.

4. Once you've written the three things down, think about *why* they happened.

5. Next, write the reasons *why* these things happened. Don't skip this either! You can write whatever you want and whatever comes naturally and easily to you. This isn't getting graded! It's just an exercise for you, and you don't have to share it with anyone for it to be helpful. Just let it flow. For example: *I got a good grade on my test because I worked hard and had support from my dad the night before when I needed to review. I got to talk to my friend during lunch because I walked over and asked them how they were doing. I got to listen to my favorite song on my way to school because I remembered to bring my headphones and listened to my favorite playlist on the bus.*

6. Write three things down every night for two weeks and notice how you feel. Or you could do this once a week for six weeks and also see beneficial results.

☺ **Happy pro tip**: You don't have to stop after a week. Keep doing this exercise as long as you'd like. The more you focus on positive experiences, the happier you'll feel!

WRITE GRATITUDE LETTERS. Another great gratitude booster is writing gratitude letters. This is easy, but powerful. All you have to do is write a letter expressing thanks to someone you appreciate and deliver it to them in person. Or for those who live far away, you can read it to them over the phone or video chat. Here's how:

1. Think about someone who did something for you that you are extremely grateful for. This could be a family member, friend, teacher, or coach. Try to pick someone you would be able to meet with in person or be able to call over the phone in the next week.

2. Now, write a letter to this person that includes the following:

- Address the person: **"Dear _____"**

- Describe in detail what this person did, why you are grateful to this person, and how this person helped you. Try to be as specific as possible.

- Describe how much it meant to you and how you remember their efforts, gift, or actions.

- Don't worry about grammar or spelling, it's the thought that counts! And try to make it at least a page long.

3. Next, you should try to deliver your letter in person, following these steps:

- Plan a visit with the person you wrote the letter to. Let that person know you'd like to see them and have something special to share, but don't reveal the exact purpose of your meeting.

- When you meet, let the person know that you are grateful to them and would like to read a letter expressing your gratitude.

- Take your time reading the letter. While you read, pay attention to their reaction as well as your own.

- Remember to give the letter to the person before you leave.

- If physical distance keeps you from making a visit, you can plan a phone or video chat.

CREATE A GRATITUDE TRAIN. Sometimes kids have a hard time identifying things they feel grateful for in their lives. I get it. This makes a lot of sense because, as you've learned, your brain is wired to identify what's wrong in your environment to keep you safe. So the trick is to think about the small things that make a difference in your life and how so many things had to come together to make them happen. I call this exercise the **Gratitude Train.** Here's how to do it!

1. Think about one small thing you liked about your day.
   - For example, *I liked the blueberry muffin I had for breakfast this morning.*

2. Now, think about what needed to happen for that thing to be available to you today or for that experience to happen at all.
   - *My mom or dad had to buy it at the store and bring it home for us to have.*

3. Next, think about what needed to happen for step 2 to occur.

- *A clerk at the store had to stock the shelves with muffins so they were available to buy.*

4. Then, what needed to happen for step 3 to occur?

- *A delivery truck had to take the muffins from the factory to the supermarket for them to stock the shelves.*

5. And, what needed to happen for step 4 to occur?

- *A baker showed up to work to make the muffins so the delivery driver could take them to the supermarket for us to buy and enjoy this morning.*

6. Did anything else need to happen for what you mentioned in the last step to occur?

- *A farmer raised chickens to collect the eggs and cows to get the milk to have the right ingredients the baker needed to make the muffins...*

Challenge yourself and keep trying to think about things that needed to happen for you to experience that small thing you enjoyed in your day. Follow the

Gratitude Train all the way to the end to highlight and remember that so many good things had to happen for even small pleasures to be part of your life. Now this leads us to another powerful feeling, **Hope.**

HOPE IS BELIEVING GOOD THINGS WILL HAPPEN IN YOUR LIFE. This means that when you *want something* and *believe that it will happen*, you feel hopeful. Hope also means that you believe that your future will be positive and fulfilling.

Researchers have discovered that feeling hopeful:

- Increases your happiness levels
- Improves your academic achievement (meaning better grades)
- Boosts your circulation and respiratory systems
- Improves your cardiovascular health (healthy heart)

There are ways to boost Hope. Ready for some more **Feel-Good Hacks**?

DREAM BOARD.

My favorite **Feel-Good Hack** for boosting hope is making a dream board. A dream board is a collage of images, pictures, quotes, and affirmations of your personal dreams and desires. Dream boards are a great source of inspiration because they remind you of the things you'd like to accomplish someday. When you are reminded of your goals and dreams, you feel hopeful. Now it's time to dream! Here's how:

1. Gather some supplies. You'll need:

   - A poster board or cork board
   - Paper
   - Tape or glue stick
   - Scissors
   - Magazines, flyers, catalogs, newspapers, stickers
   - Pictures, drawings, or photos of things and people that make you happy
   - A printer to print out inspirational quotes images from online websites, if you have access to one

2. Think about your hopes and dreams. Think about things you want to accomplish, places you'd like to go, and people that you picture being part of your life.

3. Search for images and quotes that remind you of these dreams. Cut out those things and put them aside to make your dream board collage.

4. Place your images, quotes, and pictures on your board to make an inspiring collage.

5. Once you're done, place the collage somewhere visible, that you will see daily. This helps you not only remember your dreams but also stay hopeful.

But what if you try some of these Feel-Good Hacks and still don't feel good?

GREAT QUESTION! Remember how at the beginning of this chapter we talked about how life is a rollercoaster? It's OK to not feel good all the time, even when you try. What helps the most in these moments is to remember that just like positive emotions, negative emotions are normal and temporary, and that problems have many solutions to them. A helpful personal mantra of mine is, "everything is figure-out-able." I even have a wooden plaque in my office reminding me of this every day!

This statement has helped me remember that all problems have many possible solutions and that I can always try to change the way I see a situation to figure it out. It also reminds me to have an **internal locus of control** and focus on what *I can* do to change the situation and feel better.

When you're feeling stuck, take a moment to think about what you need, and you can:

- ask for help from someone you trust,
- use a Chill-Out Hack to support you being able to think more clearly about the situation at hand, and
- remind yourself that like all the problems you have tackled before this one, you'll try your best to find a solution.

Now you're ready to problem-solve and find an alternative solution, knowing that you have control over the events that happen in your life (**Internal Locus of Control**)!

QUEST
MY FEEL-GOOD PLAN

For your final Level 8 quest you will put together a plan to increase feel-good emotions and in particular those two powerful emotions, **Hope** and **Gratitude**, in your life this week. Grab a piece of paper and pick which Feel-Good Hacks you'd like to practice and note how you feel once you're done.

The Feel-Good Hack I will practice this week is:

_____

My options are:
- 3 Good Things
- Gratitude Letter
- Gratitude Train
- Dream Board

This Feel-Good Hack is meant to increase the amount of **Gratitude** and/or **Hope** I feel.

LEVEL UP

SKILLS LEARNED

You don't have to feel happy all the time to feel good about your life. All emotions are helpful for you to enjoy life and live confidently.

Happiness is not a goal, it's a temporary feeling. (like all emotions!). All emotions are OK and expected to show up because they provide information about what you need or need to do in a particular situation.

Happiness is **feeling joy and positivity**. To feel good, you need to experience more feel-good emotions in your daily life and also feel content and satisfied with your choices and accomplishments.

Feeling good is a **skill,** and you have the ability to increase how good you feel by engaging in special activities and **Feel-Good Hacks**.

 Gratitude and **Hope** are powerful emotions that help you feel good and satisfied with your life.

 Having an **Internal Locus of Control** means understanding that you have control over the events that influence your life. When you have an internal locus of control, you believe that you influence what happens in your life rather than blaming others for what happens.

GREAT WORK COMPLETING LEVEL 8! IN THE NEXT LEVEL YOU'LL LEARN ABOUT HAVING AN "I GOT THIS!" ATTITUDE TO BUILD YOUR GROWTH MINDSET AND GRIT. SEE YOU THERE!

AN "I GOT THIS!" ATTITUDE AND IDENTIFYING YOUR STRENGTHS

_R_ owan and Otto are in the same math class. On their most recent math test, they both got Cs. Their teacher, Mr. Bloom, let the class know that it was a challenging test, and the class would have the opportunity to complete some additional work for extra credit before the next test. Rowan and Otto had the following reactions to their grades and the news about the additional extra credit work...

I suck at math! There's no way I'll be able to get my grade up after this. What's the point in even doing the extra credit work?

I definitely need to study more and ask Mr. Bloom for some pointers before the next test. I'm glad he's giving us the opportunity to get some extra credit. That'll definitely help me keep my grade up!

Even though Rowan and Otto both experienced the same thing, they had very different responses and planned on approaching the situation in very different ways. Rowan decided that it was not worth the effort to do the extra credit work because they thought they were not good at math and that wouldn't change. Otto looked at his grade and decided to problem-solve how to prepare better for next time, and to take Mr. Bloom up on his offer to complete extra credit.

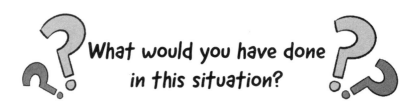

What would you have done in this situation?

THE WAY WE SEE THE WORLD AROUND US AND HOW WE BEHAVE TOWARD LIFE IS YOUR MINDSET.

The difference in response between Rowan and Otto was determined by their **Mindset**. Your Mindset is the way you think about yourself and the world around you. **Mindset** also refers to the way you think about your abilities and talents. Your mindset influences everything in your life, from how you receive feedback to whether or not you finish difficult tasks. Additionally, your Mindset is also one of the greatest factors in determining whether or not you grow and improve in your abilities throughout your life.

There are two different kinds of mindset: **Fixed Mindset** and **Growth Mindset**. People don't just have a fully Fixed or Growth Mindset. You can have both! You may have a Fixed Mindset in one area of your life and Growth Mindset in another. For example, you may have a fixed mindset about math and growth mindset about learning to play the guitar. But overall, Mindset seems pretty important, right? Let's check out the two types of Mindsets and which one will help you thrive and navigate life confidently.

People who have a FIXED MINDSET	People who have a GROWTH MINDSET
Believe that they're born with a fixed or set amount of intelligence, talent, and skill that can't change.	Understand that their skill, talent and intelligence can improve over time with effort and practice.
In other words, you're stuck with what you have!	Are more likely to embrace challenging tasks and work hard to improve.
Tend to choose easier tasks that involve little effort or feel natural and come easily to them.	View failure and mistakes as a chance to learn and grow.
Feel like it's a personal attack or an insult when someone offers them feedback.	View feedback as an opportunity to improve and develop new skills.
	View obstacles as an opportunity to experiment and solve problems in a different way.
Give up when faced with an obstacle.	Welcome creative risks, experimentation, and different ways of doing things as opportunities to innovate and improve.
Are less likely to take creative risks.	

 Which mindset do you think Rowan showed when they received their math grade? How about Otto?

If you guessed that Rowan was demonstrating a Fixed Mindset and Otto showed us a Growth Mindset response, you're right!

ROWAN'S FIXED MINDSET APPROACH:

- They felt defeated after getting a low grade on the test.

- They took this to mean that they're not good at math and that it wouldn't change even if they completed the extra credit work assigned.

- They believe that their ability to understand math is FIXED (cannot change).

- They plan on avoiding the challenge of completing the extra credit work to improve their grade because they don't want to fail again.

OTTO'S GROWTH MINDSET APPROACH:

- He acknowledged that he got a low grade and decided to problem-solve what to do differently next time to improve.

- He believed that he could learn anything with enough effort and practice.

- He embraced the challenge of completing the extra credit work Mr. Bloom assigned.

- He enjoys challenges and understands that making mistakes and effort is part of learning.

Seems that Otto understands something really important about his brain: It has the ability to change! In Level 2 you learned about your fantastic supercomputer brain and **neuroplasticity.** Your brain can grow like any other muscle in your body with practice and training. **NEUROPLASTICITY IS YOUR BRAIN'S ABILITY TO LEARN, CHANGE, AND ADAPT WITH EFFORT.** When you learn something new or have a new experience, you create new connections in your brain, and this updates your supercomputer to adapt to new circumstances and grow. This is how it works...

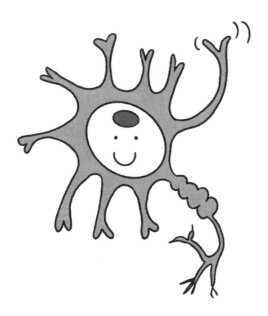

A neuron is a brain cell, and you have over a hundred BILLION neurons in your brain. Neurons are the cells that help you think. **EVERY NEW EXPERIENCE CREATES CONNECTIONS BETWEEN NEURONS.** These connections are called synapses and enable your brain to function and do what you want it to do. Think of these connections as roads being built between neurons that help you learn and grow.

When you do something for the first time, the connection between neurons will take effort and feel difficult, like trying to walk a path through a forest that hasn't been walked on before. The first connection is the hardest. It will be challenging.

With effort and practice, your neurons have connected so many times that they've gone from being a rocky road to being a smooth, paved route, and eventually your very own brilliant superhighway! When you practice something over and over your brain builds and strengthens these connections in your brain.

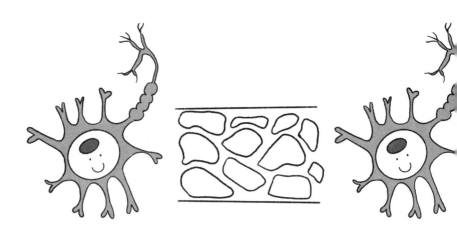

Have you ever wondered why Practice Makes Progress?

Practice makes progress because of neuroplasticity! The more you practice something like an instrument, sport, or even math, the more the connection and path between neurons improves and become easier to connect next time. Having walked that path multiple times makes your experience feel easier. This is why with practice, you make progress. Your brain is helping you create the connections you need to engage in that skill, so that next time you try, you know what to do, and continue to grow and improve.

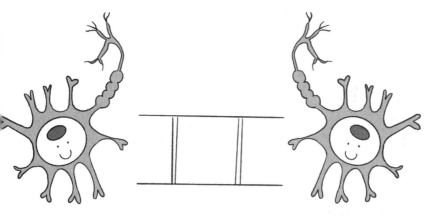

WHAT YOU THINK OF AS INTELLIGENCE AND YOUR ABILITY TO BE GOOD AT THINGS IS NOT STUCK OR PERMANENT. YOUR BRAIN CAN IMPROVE AND GROW WITH EFFORT BECAUSE OF NEUROPLASTICITY!

So, if you're finding yourself having a fixed mindset, what can you do? It really comes down to changing the way you think about or see a situation. As you now know, you can change the way you think to change the way you feel. Check out these tips on how to build your growth mindset:

HOW TO HAVE A GROWTH MINDSET

- **View challenges as opportunities.** Look for different ways to learn new things. Effort makes you stronger and smarter!

- **Choose learning things *well* over learning them fast**. Getting good at something takes time, and you have to be willing to make mistakes and stay with it.

- **Making mistakes doesn't mean you're a failure.** Making a mistake means you're on the right track, you're just not there yet. Successful people fail all the time!

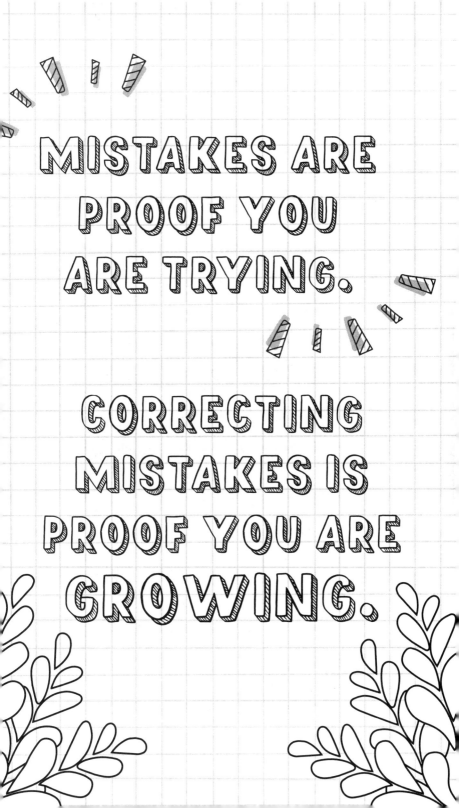

- **Learn from the mistakes of others.** Pretend it was you making the mistake and consider how you can apply this lesson to your life.

- **Learn to love feedback.** Receiving feedback is just a suggestion to work on a particular area of your life. Remember not to take feedback personally. When someone provides you with a correction or feedback, the intention is to support and teach you how to be more skilled, and that's what growing is all about. So welcome the support and don't take it as a personal attack, but rather as helpful guidance to get better!

- **Set a new goal for every accomplishment that you achieve.** Goals help you stay motivated. There's always another goal to reach or project to tackle.

YOU CAN CHANGE YOUR MINDSET WITH YOUR WORDS!

INSTEAD OF THINKING THIS ...	THINK THIS...
I can't do this.	With some feedback and support from others, I can get this done.
I give up. I'll never get it.	I need to make an effort and not let myself give up. I just need to find the right strategy or ask for help.
This is way too hard.	This IS hard, and if I keep working at it, I will figure it out.
This is way too easy.	How can I make this better?
I'm just not good at this.	I haven't figured this out YET, but I will learn.
I don't want to make a mistake.	Mistakes are OK, expected when learning new things, and will help me figure out what works.
This is good enough.	Did I try my hardest? How can I improve it?

What if I told you that there is one other personal trait that is one of the BIGGEST predictors of personal success? That trait is...

GIVE IT YOUR ALL

RE-DO IF YOU HAVE TO

IGNORE WANTING TO GIVE UP

TAKE TIME TO DO IT RIGHT

You have **GRIT** when you are able to work towards your goals without giving up or letting obstacles stand in the way. Even when it gets hard, you keep at it. This is a trait of people who are perseverant and fully dedicated to their goals. Gritty people know that mistakes and setbacks are expected. They also know that working hard is necessary to get what you want.

The good news is that being gritty, like growth mindset, is a skill and can be learned, and there are several things that you can do to build your grit.

HOW TO CULTIVATE GRIT

- **Remember that your skills grow with effort.** When faced with a challenging assignment or task, remind yourself that you need to stick with it and not give up. Using positive, can-do self-talk such as, *I believe in myself, I will get this, I just need to keep trying, and I know I can problem-solve my way through this*, will help make you grittier!

- **Embrace failing and making mistakes.** To accomplish personal goals, you will encounter setbacks and obstacles along the way. When you learn anything new, you're likely to make mistakes. That's just how it is! Gritty people embrace mistakes because they understand that mistakes help you learn, teach you about what does not work, and help you grow.

- **Reward yourself.** When you're working towards big goals with perseverance and dedication, the task can feel really big, so it's easy to get discouraged. When you break your goal down into smaller parts and reward yourself for accomplishing each small step, you will be able to celebrate your progress and are more likely to stay motivated to accomplish your goals.

Grit and **Growth Mindset** are related and support each other. For example, when you have a Growth Mindset, you expect that your abilities can be improved with effort and practice, and that effort and practice takes hard work. When you have grit and stick with it, it strengthens your Growth Mindset because you can see that your efforts lead to improvement in a skill or area of knowledge. So, next time you take on a challenge, remember to work on both your growth mindset and grit to help you accomplish your goals!

THE POWER OF MISTAKES

We talked a lot about mistakes just now, but let's focus in even more. Mistakes are an important part of building your growth mindset and grit, and of growing as a person. When you make a mistake, your brain grows. How? There are connections that happen in your brain that can only happen when you make a mistake. It's true! When you make a mistake, you think harder, and this is when your brain grows the most. When you get something right the first time, these connections don't occur, and your brain doesn't grow as much. This is why it's so important to work hard and embrace challenges so you can make mistakes, learn, and grow.

So always remember:

MISTAKES ARE...

NECESSARY FOR LEARNING

OPPORTUNITIES TO GET BETTER AND GROW

EXPECTED, RESPECTED, INSPECTED, AND CORRECTED!

To be ready to take on mistakes and grow your brilliant brain, it's helpful to know your **Strengths.** There are so many wonderful and unique things about you. You have qualities that not everyone has. These are your strengths. Personal strengths are qualities you possess and actions you do well. Strengths can include your skills (including cognitive, social, and emotional skills), talents, and knowledge. You can use your personal strengths to achieve your goals with confidence. Let's get to know your unique strengths!

Quest
MEET YOUR STRENGTHS

To find your strengths, it's helpful to know what you enjoy doing, because those are usually things you have spent time on and are good at. Grab a piece of paper and something to write with. Take a look at the list below and write down all the things you like. There might be things that you like that aren't on the list, and that's OK. This list is just to get you to started. Go ahead and write down other things, too.

- Playing sports
- Cooking
- Baking
- Reading
- Writing
- Finance and business
- Coding
- Music
- Animals
- Video games
- Watching sports
- Working out
- Yoga
- Biking
- Hanging out with friends
- Volunteering and helping others
- Playing board games
- Hiking
- Connecting with your family

Now, let's identify your strengths. Often, you can't see your strengths for yourself. But those who know you well are able to notice things you excel at. These are the things they've witnessed you doing when you're at your best. For this quest...

1. Ask three people that you care about to share three things that they know you're really good at. These people can be people you respect, like family members, teachers, friends, or mentors. Write down the unique strengths they share with you.

2. Now that you have your list provided by others, go ahead and picture yourself at your best, when you're doing something you love, or inspired and working towards your goals. What qualities do you show in those moments? Brainstorm a list of traits that you like about yourself. You can use the list on the next page for inspiration or you can come up with your own.

3. Now pick the top five that are most important to you. List them on a piece of paper or in the notes on your phone to remember your personal gifts, and remember them when you're working towards personal goals.

Good Friend

Gritty

Thoughtful

CONSISTENT

CREATIVE

Honest

Considerate

Perseverant

HARD-WORKING

FUNNY

FLEXiBLe

BRAVE

Curious

DETERMINED

Grateful

Loyal

Patient

TRUSTWORTHY

Friendly

DEDICATED

Kind

Mini Quest
EMBRACE MISTAKES

Grab a piece of paper and something to write with. Think about a time you thought you made a mistake. This mistake could be big or small, and could have happened at school, on the field, at home, or with your friends.

1. Describe a mistake you made.

2. Think about what you LEARNED from this mistake. Describe it (in writing!).

3. What will you do differently next time *because* you made this mistake? Write this down, too.

4. How did this mistake help you grow? Write this last bit, too. ☺

LEVEL UP

SKILLS LEARNED

 Your **MINDSET** is the way you see the world around you and how you behave towards life. You can have a fixed or a growth mindset.

 A **fixed mindset** is when you believe that you're born with your abilities (either born artistic or not, smart or not smart), and think they can't change. People with a fixed mindset avoid challenging themselves and fear making mistakes.

 A **growth mindset** is when you believe that your abilities can be improved with effort and practice (you can get smarter or better at art). People with a growth mindset embrace failure and mistakes because they know these are opportunities to learn and grow.

Grit is a personal trait of people who are able to work towards their goals, not give up, and overcome obstacles, even when it gets hard. Grit is highly associated with personal success.

 Mistakes are expected, respected, inspected, and corrected!

NICE JOB! YOU JUST LEARNED HOW TO BUILD YOUR GROWTH MINDSET, GRIT, EMBRACE YOUR MISTAKES, AND GET TO KNOW YOUR PERSONAL STRENGTHS. KEEP IT UP! ON THE NEXT AND FINAL LEVEL, YOU'LL LEARN HOW TO PUT ALL YOUR NEW STRESS MANAGEMENT SKILLS TOGETHER TO UPDATE YOUR BRAIN SUPERCOMPUTER SOFTWARE. SEE YOU THERE.

UPDATE YOUR
SOFTWARE

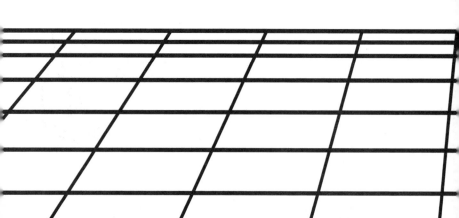

*Y*ou made it! Congratulations on making it to Level 10, the final level in your stress management journey. You've learned so much already! To complete the final level, let's first review all the skills you've learned so far:

LEVEL 1

Stress is normal! Stress is your body's natural response to keep you safe. There is good and bad stress, but remember: **When stress is messing stuff up, it's time to level up!**

LEVEL 2

Your brain is a supercomputer that can change and adapt to new experiences. CBT offers strategies to level up your stress management skills. **What you think, you feel, you do!**

LEVEL 3

Your daily habits impact how you think and feel. Good nutrition is important and should include all food groups. Remember: **Move your body every day and eat the rainbow!**

LEVEL 4

Chill-Out Hacks help you feel relaxed and in control. You can use Physical or Breathing Chill-Out Hacks to keep your cool when you need it most. Remember:
Mindful > Mind FULL

LEVEL 5

To be brave you have to feel scared. Fear is often a sign you're doing something new or taking on a challenge that will help you grow.

Formula for bravery:
1. Do not let fear call the shots
2. Tolerate feeling scared with the help of Chill-Out Hacks
3. Face your fears using a Bravery Ladder

LEVEL 6

Your amazing brain makes mistakes. You can catch these **Brain Mistakes** and challenge them to support thinking more clearly. You can use a thought log to help you.

A general rule to challenge a Brain Mistake is:
What advice would I give to a friend who had this same thought?

LEVEL 7

Emotion Smarts is your ability to understand and use your emotions effectively. **You can use the following strategies and tools to continue to build your Emotion Smarts:**

Body Clues Emotions Chart	Offer & Seek Validation
Feelings Chart	HALT
I-Statements	

LEVEL 8

Feeling good is a skill and you have the ability to increase it by using your **FEEL-GOOD HACKS.** Having an **INTERNAL LOCUS OF CONTROL** means that you influence what happens in your life!

LEVEL 9

When you have a **GROWTH MINDSET,** you understand that your abilities are able to improve with effort and practice. **GRIT,** highly associated with personal success, means that you don't give up on your goals, no matter how hard it gets.

FINAL LEVEL UP CHALLENGE:
Update your mental software
by using all the skills you've learned.

It has been AWESOME getting to be your coach throughout this journey. We all need a little help sometimes, don't we? For your last Level, I wanted to teach you how to be your OWN stress management coach.

SELF-TALK

Have you ever noticed that you are having conversations in your head throughout the day? I'm sure you have! This is normal—we all have conversations with ourselves in our head all day long. In fact, scientists have discovered on average we have 6,200 thoughts per day. That's a lot of information to go through! Many of these thoughts are **Self-Talk**, the thoughts we have *about* ourselves, when referring *to* ourselves. Self-Talk is your internal dialogue. There are two different types of self-talk: negative and positive.

LET'S MEET YOUR INNER CRITIC, A.K.A. YOUR NEGATIVE SELF-TALK. Sometimes you might notice a thought that comes up for you that's unhelpful or hurtful. Thoughts like these that Otto is having:

I'm not smart enough.

This is too hard.

I can't do this.

This is too scary.

No one likes me.

I'll never get my work done.

I always mess stuff up!

I won't be able to figure this out, it's too hard.

Negative self-talk happens to all of us, and these thoughts can contain unkind beliefs that are not based on facts and are not true. **SELF-TALK LIKE THIS IS YOUR INNER CRITIC TALKING.** Like a critic, this kind of self-talk has lots of opinions that are often unhelpful, judgmental, and unwelcome. Your inner critic can really mess stuff up sometimes because you might start believing that these things are true and that maybe there's something wrong with you. Negative self-talk can make you feel stressed, sad, worried, and down on yourself. Often your inner critic chatter also makes you feel like not trying new things or even avoiding things throughout the day.

I think I know the answer, but I know I'll get it wrong. I'll just not raise my hand and hope Mr. B doesn't call on me.

There's no way I'll be good enough to help my team beat them. This team's won every game this season. I'm going to mess up. What's the point?!

Do you notice your inner critic brain chatter? What does that self-talk say to you?

Luckily, there's something you can do when your inner critic is trying to mess stuff up for you. You can call on your inner coach to help you out!

MEET YOUR INNER COACH (POSITIVE SELF-TALK).
Have you ever helped yourself through a tough time by telling yourself, "I got this! I can do this. I am strong"? Positive self-talk is when you speak to yourself kindly, in a supportive voice, and in a way that challenges negative thinking and predictions. That's your inner coach showing up! Your inner coach can help you reconsider how you look at situations and challenges. Your inner coach does this by providing you with thoughts that are helpful, loving, and remind you of your personal strengths. Your inner coach uses facts about yourself to help you when you need it. Because your inner coach thinks about your inner strengths and past experiences of bravery, its beliefs about you are almost always true. When your inner coach is in

charge of your thoughts, you will feel supported, confident, calm, and ready to take on any challenge.

I think I know the answer but I'm not sure. I'll raise my hand and try to respond to Mr. B since I know I studied last night and remember this topic. Even if I get it wrong, Mr. B won't make me feel bad about it. Other students give wrong answers all the time and nothing bad happens. I'll go ahead and try.

The team we're playing today is great! They haven't lost a game this season. This is a great opportunity for me and my team to show them what we got. Let's do this!

Your inner coach is there to motivate and cheer you on. The thoughts from your inner coach help you stay positive and hopeful. Like other coaches, your inner coach will also be there to support you and help you come up with a game plan when things get hard. It will remind you that mistakes are expected and that you can always try again. Your coach knows you well and believes in you, no matter what.

The great thing about your inner coach is that you can always ask for support when you need it. If you find yourself using negative self-talk and your inner critic is trying to put you down, all you have to do is remember to ask yourself what your inner coach would say, as Otto is doing...

Otto came up with:

This is really hard, but I'll ask for help and try my best.

I haven't figured this out, yet!

I will stick with it and not give up!

I'm fun to spend time with.

I can do hard things.

What can I do to enjoy myself when friends are not available?

I can always ask for help when I need it.

I will make a plan and work on it one step at a time.

I made a mistake. Mistakes are expected and help me learn what works and what doesn't work. Let's try that again.

Mini Quest

POWER CARDS

Power Cards are a tool to help you remember to call on your inner coach for support whenever you need it. The strategy is simple.

- ○ Grab some index cards or small pieces of paper and something to write with.

- ○ Think about what your inner coach might say to you in different situations.

- ○ Write one positive self-talk statement on each card that you find helpful and makes you feel powerful and strong.

- ○ Keep your Power Cards next to your bed or backpack or other private space to read before bed or anytime your inner critic is trying to interfere. You could also keep them in the notes app on your phone, or in a document on your computer.

- ○ Try to choose at least five positive self-talk statements to add to your power card stack. You can use quotes from songs, movies, or your favorite athlete or mentor too, if you find that inspiring.

POSITIVE SELF-TALK AND QUOTES

I GOT THIS!

"" I CAN DO HARD THINGS. ""

What would a good friend tell me about this situation?

"" What advice would I give a good friend who was going through this? ""

"" I can choose to be calm in this situation by using a Chill-Out Hack. ""

" Challenges make me grow. They are not easy, but they are worth it!

Giving up is the only sure way to fail.

" This is figure-out-able.

"" I LEARN FROM ALL MY MISTAKES. ""

Once I stay in an anxiety-causing situation long enough, I will get used to it and it will become easier.

> **"** I am not where I want to be, YET! **"**

I've survived 100% of all the difficulties I've experienced.

What would someone with strong confidence think or do in this situation?

I can accomplish anything with effort and persistence. I can be gritty!

> **"** "Great things come from hard work and perseverance. No excuses."
> —Kobe Bryant, Professional Basketball Player, MVP **"**

> **"** "Nothing is impossible. The word itself says 'I'M POSSIBLE.'"
> —Audrey Hepburn, Actress **"**

> **"** "I have not failed. I've just found 10,000 ways that won't work." —Thomas Edison, Inventor **"**

"Do the best you can until you know better. Then when you know better, do better."
—Maya Angelou, Author & Rights Activist

"You just can't beat the person who won't give up." —Babe Ruth, Baseball player

"Before you conquer the mountain, you must learn to overcome your fear."
—Isabel Allende, Author

"Would you like me to give you a formula for success? It's quite simple, really. Double your rate of failure."
—Thomas Watson, Businessman

"Everything you want is on the other side of fear." —Jack Canfield, Author

"BOSS UP AND CHANGE YOUR LIFE."
—Lizzo, Singer, Rapper, Songwriter, and Flutist

"Try a thing you haven't done three times. Once, to get over the fear of doing it. Twice, to learn how to do it. And a third time, to figure out whether you like it or not." —Virgil Garnett Thomson, Composer

"Courage is like a muscle. We strengthen it when we use it." —Ruth Gordon, Actress, Screenwriter & Playwright

"The expert at anything was once a beginner."—Helen Hayes, Actress

YOUR POWER CARD STACK CAN GROW OVER TIME. EVERY TIME YOU CAN THINK OF A POWERFUL THOUGHT, QUOTE, OR STATEMENT, ADD IT TO YOUR POWER CARDS PACK!

YOUR STRESS PLAN

Now you're fully equipped to support yourself when stress feels overwhelming. You can count on the strategies you've learned in this book, and you also know how to continue being your very own supportive coach. Now let's discuss what you will choose to incorporate in your stress management plan to move forward confidently knowing that you have all the tools you need.

Let's see how the players have implemented their stress management plans for inspiration:

Rowan makes sure to exercise regularly, eat healthy meals throughout the day, and do stretches while listening to a guided meditation every night to transition to a good night's sleep. They also ask themselves, "what would I say to a friend who had this same thought?" so they can consistently respond to situations more kindly and effectively as well as support reframing any brain mistakes that come up.

Luna uses her journal to write down brain mistakes that came up during her day and uses the thought record to make sure to challenge these unhelpful thoughts. When communicating with others, Luna uses her I-statements and emotion chart to make sure she's helping others understand her needs and support her when she needs it. Luna also checks in with her HALT strategy (hungry, angry, lonely, or tired) when she's not feeling her best in order to address these needs before moving forward.

Otto and his family share three good things that happened or practice the gratitude train at dinner every night. He also reads his power statements in the morning before school and before going to bed to remind himself of his strengths and start and end his day confidently. Otto builds on his growth mindset and grit often by trying new things and remembering to view challenges as opportunities and mistakes as expected and helpful.

 How are you going to use your stress management skills?

QUEST
UPDATE YOUR SOFTWARE

Your turn! Time to update your stress software.

1. Grab a piece of paper and something to write with.

2. Write down a stress management plan for yourself by answering these questions:

- What is an area of my life that is causing me stress right now? Is it school, homework, after-school activities, family, or friend stuff? Or a little of everything?

- Which strategy can I use to help me with this? (Review earlier Levels for inspiration.)

- Who is going to be part of my tech support team? Could I ask my parents, mentors, teachers, counselor, friends, siblings, or family members to be on my team?

- How am I going to do these strategies? Do I need to schedule a time in the day to complete them? Do I need to ask my support team to make sure I follow through with my plan?

- What is my plan for completion? Are there things I can do daily or weekly?

3. Once you have determined your plan (and any steps) be sure to add it to your planner. This will help you get things done and be consistent enough to create a habit.

You did it! You've finished your last level and are ready to take on middle school and beyond confidently, with all the stress management skills you need to succeed. When you feel stressed or overwhelmed, remember to come back to the tools in this book to figure out what to do next. You have everything you need to manage stressful times. It's up to you to put all this knowledge into practice in your life to see the benefits they can provide.

You should feel so proud! Remember that these resources are available to you any time you need them. Come back often and remember, you've got this! **YOU KNOW HOW TO TAKE ON STRESSFUL SITUATIONS LIKE THE CONFIDENT KID YOU ARE!** Until next time.

With gratitude,
Coach Silvi

Extra Resources

Below is a list of other books and online resources that can further help you and your parents. Take a look to see which ones stand out to you or might help you most with topics that can be challenging.

RECOMMENDED BOOKS FOR TWEENS AND TEENS

Alvord, M. K., & McGrath, A. (2017). *Conquer negative thinking for teens: A workbook to break the nine thought habits that are holding you back.* New Harbinger Publications.

Battistin, J. M.& Owen, C. (2019). *Mindfulness for teens in 10 minutes a day : Exercises to feel calm, stay focused & be your best self.* Rockridge Press.

Berman, J. (2021). *Self-regulation workbook for kids: CBT exercises and coping strategies to help children handle anxiety, stress, and other strong emotions.* Ulysses Press.

Bernstein, J. (2019). *The stress survival guide for teens : CBT skills to worry less, develop grit, & live your best life.* Instant Help Book.

Covey, S. (2014). *The 7 habits of highly effective teens.* Touchstone.

Dewar, M. D. (2021). *The mindful breathing workbook for teens : Simple practices to help you manage stress and feel better now.* New Harbinger Publications.

Goff, S. (2021). *Brave : A teen girl's guide to beating worry and anxiety.* Bethany House.

Halloran, J. (2020). *Coping skills for teens workbook : 60 helpful ways to deal with stress, anxiety and anger.* Encourage Play LLC.

Hurley, K. (2020). *A year of positive thinking for teens : Daily motivation to beat stress, inspire happiness, and achieve your goals.* Rockridge Press.

Hutt, R. L. (2019). *Feeling better : CBT workbook for teens : Essential skills and activities to help you manage moods, boost self-esteem, and conquer anxiety.* Althea Press.

McCloud, C., & Messing, D. (2016). *Have you filled a bucket today? : A guide to daily happiness for kids.* Partners Publishing Group.

Napawan, A. (2021). *Happiness workbook: A CBT-based guide to foster positivity and embrace joy.* Rockridge Press.

Schleider, J. L., Mullarkey, M. C., & Dobias, M. L. (2021). *The growth mindset workbook for teens : Say yes to challenges, deal with difficult emotions, and reach your full potential.* Instant Help Books.

RECOMMENDED FICTION BOOKS FOR TWEENS AND TEENS

Craft, J. (2019). *New kid.* Quill Tree Books.

Patterson, J. (2012). *Middle school, the worst years of my life (Middle School, 1).* Jimmy Patterson.

Reynolds, J. (2021). *Stuntboy, in the meantime*. Atheneum/Caitlyn Dlouhy Books.

Telgemeier, R. (2017). *Guts: A graphic novel*. Graphix.

Telgemeier, R. (2020). *Smile: A graphic novel*. Graphix.

RECOMMENDED BOOKS FOR PARENTS AND ADULT CAREGIVERS

Alvord, M. K., Grados, J. J., & Zucker, B. (2011). *Resilience builder program for children and adolescents: Enhancing social competence and self-regulation: A cognitive -behavioral approach*. Research Press.

Icard, M. (2021). *Fourteen talks by age fourteen: The essential conversations you need to have with your kids before they start high school*. Harmony.

Koplewicz, H. S. (2021). *The scaffold effect: Raising resilient, self-reliant, and secure kids in an age of anxiety*. Harmony.

Morin, A. (2018). *13 things mentally strong parents don't do: Raising self-assured children and training their brains for a life of happiness, meaning, and success*. William Morrow Paperbacks.

Siegel, D. J. (2013). *Brainstorm: The power and purpose of the teenage brain*. Jeremy P. Tarcher Perigee.

Siegel, D. J., & Bryson, T. P. (2019). *The yes brain: How to cultivate courage, curiosity, and resilience in your child*. Bantam.

Stixrud, W., & Johnson, N. (2019). *The self-driven child: The science and sense of giving your kids more control over their lives*. Penguin Books.

Stixrud, W., & Johnson, N. (2021). *What do you say? How to talk with kids to build motivation, stress tolerance, and a happy home*. Viking.

Zucker, B. (2016). *Anxiety-free kids: An interactive guide for parents and children*. Routledge.

VIDEOS AND PODCASTS

PODCASTS:

Being 12 Podcast: The Year Everything Changes. (2015). [Audio podcast]. WNYC. https://www.wnyc.org/series/being-12/

Big Life Journal (Producer) (2019-present). *Big life kids podcast—A growth mindset podcast for kids* [Audio podcast]. Big Life Journal. https://biglifejournal.com/pages/podcast

Damour, L. (Host). 2019, May. Anxiety and teen girls (No. 80). *In Speaking of Psychology*. American Psychological Association. https://www.apa.org/research/action/speaking-of-psychology/anxiety-teen-girls

Smith, C., Daniels, M., & Beard, M. (Hosts). (2019–present). *Short & Curly* [Audio podcast]. Big Life Journal. https://www.abc.net.au/radio/programs/shortandcurly/

VIDEOS:

Cain, S. (2012,).*The power of introverts* [Video]. Ted Conferences. https://www.ted.com/talks/susan_cain_the_power_of_introverts

Cuddy, A. (2012). *Your body language may shape who you are* [Video]. TED Conferences. https://www.ted.com/talks/amy_cuddy_your_body_language_may_shape_who_you_are

Duckworth, A. L. (n.d.) *Grit: The power of passion and perseverance* [Video]. TED Conferences. https://www.ted.com/talks/angela_lee_duckworth_grit_the_power_of_passion_and_perseverance/

Dweck, C. (2014, December 17). *The power of believing that you can improve | Carol Dweck*. [Video]. YouTube. https://www.youtube.com/watch?v=_XomgOOSpLU

Galván, A.. (2013, February 13). *Insight Into the Teenage Brain: Adriana Galván at TEDxYouth@Caltech*. [Video]. YouTube. https://www.youtube.com/watch?v=LWUkW4s3XxY

Saujani, R. (2016). *Teach girls bravery, not perfection* [Video]. TED Conferences. https://www.ted.com/talks/reshma_saujani_teach_girls_bravery_not_perfection

Soulpancake. (2013, July 11). *An experiment in gratitude* [Video]. YouTube. https://www.youtube.com/watch?v=oHv6vTKD6lg

Soulpancake (2013, January 23). *A pep talk from kid president to you* [Video]. YouTube. https://www.youtube.com/watch?v=l-gQLqv9f4o&t=35s

Urban, T. (2016). *Inside the mind of a master procrastinator* [Video]. TED Conferences. https://www.ted.com/talks/tim_urban_inside_the_mind_of_a_master_procrastinator

Willard, C. (2016, September 28). *Growing up Stressed or Growing up Mindful? | Christopher Willard | TEDxYouth@GDRHS*. [Video]. YouTube. https://www.youtube.com/watch?v=znlsoaM_ALQ

Winkler, M. (n.d.). *What makes a hero?* [Video] TED Conferences. https://ed.ted.com/lessons/what-makes-a-hero-matthew-winkler

ONLINE RESOURCES

The following websites provide information and videos that offer useful tips.

CHANGE TO CHILL BY ALLINA HEALTH

https://www.changetochill.org/

Change to Chill offers free online mental health resources for teens designed to help them learn how to relax and integrate healthy habits into their lifestyle.

GoZen

https://gozen.com/

This subscription-based program suite teaches children ages 6-15 essential social and emotional learning skills through animated stories and interactive practice. Programs offered are all about helping kids thrive by transforming their worry and other tough emotions into skills of resilience.

SOULPANCAKE

https://participant.com/soulpancake

SoulPancake was created to encourage open-hearted dialogue about what it means to be human. Website content explores the ways we all seek connection, hope, truth, identity, and purpose.

THE BOUNCE BACK PROJECT: PROMOTING HEALTH THROUGH HAPPINESS.

https://www.feelinggoodmn.org/what-we-do/bounce-back-project-/

This initiative from CentraCare Health offers information and ideas on the five pillars of resilience.

WHOLEHEARTED SCHOOL COUNSELING

https://wholeheartedschoolcounseling.com/

Trauma-informed and solution-focused resource maker for educators, parents, and students that focuses on social-emotional learning, coping skills, and student success.

DIY AND JOURNALING RESOURCES

If you are looking for additional writing prompts, journaling activities, or workbooks, here are several excellent resources:

Battistin, J. M. (2019). *The mindfulness journal for teens: Prompts and practices to help you stay cool, calm, and present*. Rockridge Press.

Big Life Journal. (2018). *Big life journal—Teen edition: A growth mindset journal*.

Cogan, C. & Smith, H. (2021). *Creating calm—Journal for teens: Journal therapy for calming anxiety and understanding the teenage brain*. Independently published.

Gratitude Daily. (2020). *The ultimate middle school gratitude journal: Thinking big and thriving in middle school with 100 days of gratitude, daily journal prompts and inspirational quotes*. Creative Ideas Publishing.

Journal Buddies. (2022). *Journal prompts for teens (and tweens)*. https://www.journalbuddies.com/journal-prompts-writing-ideas/journal-prompts-for-teens/

Liem, C. & Liem, A. (2020). *Happy mindset little journal: Kids interactive journal prompts and daily activities to help children develop a growth mindset*. Thrive Print Co.

MOBILE APPS

Sometimes an app can really help; so many kids find it natural to use an app to process emotions, track their schedules, or get into a relaxed state. Apps can help cue you to take steps toward a goal, such as tracking your bravery missions, movement habits, and doing a daily gratitude practice. Take a look at the list below and try one out; you may also recommend one to the grown-ups in your life.

Antistress. This subscription-based app offers relaxing toys and games to engage with when you need to chill.

Bear in Mind. This app will help you create to-do lists and set up reminders to keep you on track with daily goals.

CBT Thought Diary. This subscription-based app uses a scientific approach to journaling, which allows you to track your mood and identify faulty thinking patterns and emotions. It uses effective tools from Cognitive Behavioral Therapy (CBT), Acceptance and Commitment Therapy (ACT), Dialectical Behavioral Therapy (DBT), and Positive Psychology to help improve your mood.

Choiceworks Calendar. This paid app is a great assistive technology tool that can alleviate the anxiety some kids associate with schedule changes. This app offers a picture-based learning tool that helps you learn what is happening day-to-day, week-to-week, and month-to-month throughout each year. It teaches the abstract concept of time in a structured visual format, which helps children organize their lives as well as understand sequence and time. This app provides a full-featured calendar designed with both the child and caregiver in mind.

Chore Pad. This productivity app lets families set their own tasks or chores and supports creating a reward system based on completion.

Habitica. This is a free habit-building and productivity app that treats your real life like a game. With in-game rewards and punishments to motivate you and a strong social network to inspire you, it can help you achieve your goals to become healthy, hard-working, and happy.

Habitz. This fun to use app empowers you to develop healthy habits and stick to them.

Happify. Learn and practice activities that can help you combat negativity, anxiety, and stress while fostering positive traits like gratitude and empathy.

Happy Not Perfect. This app offers mind workouts, daily affirmations, and meditations to help you build confidence, manage stress, and promote sleep.

Insight Timer. Thousands of different meditations, relaxing imagery and sounds, and guided practices, including ones specifically for anxiety and for bedtime, are offered on this free app.

Stop, Breathe, and Think. This subscription-based app helps you create a daily meditation practice and has meditations, journaling, videos, and even yoga lessons.

Smiling Mind. This not-for-profit guided meditation app was developed by psychologists and educators to help bring mindfulness into your life. It provides helpful instructional videos as well as programs customized by age that can be used in a variety of settings where one can benefit from mindfulness practice (home, school, work, sports, sleep, etc.).

Streaks. This app helps you form or break habits and supports daily tracking by encouraging you not to break your streak.

Superbetter. This mobile game is designed to improve the player's mental health and build resilience. It aims to help the user track their goals and achievements, while also providing education about the importance of each activity.

Woebot. This free app is grounded in clinical research and powered by Artificial Intelligence. It helps you develop skills to challenge your thinking and build healthy habits. Think through situations with step-by-step guidance using proven therapeutic frameworks like Cognitive Behavioral Therapy (CBT).

Acknowledgments

I'd like to thank Dr. Bonnie Zucker for the opportunity to collaborate on this inspired project to support children and their families through an exciting time of transition, growth, and change. I am eternally grateful for your generous spirit, wisdom, mentorship, and friendship. You are the truest example of a consummate and compassionate human being supporting others in this world. Thank you for setting an example of what it means to commit to your dreams, work hard, and never give up on the things that set your heart and soul on fire.

This book series would not have been possible if it wasn't for Kristine Enderle and Katie ten Hagen's vision, creativity, and commitment to providing the highest quality resources for children and teens. Thank you for trusting me with this book, for believing in my vision, ideas, and for always being such a positive source of guidance and support. Thank you to Julie Spalding, Rachel Ross, and Deandra Hodge for your dedication to this series.

I am grateful for my co-authors in this series, Dr. Lenka Glassman, Dr. Anna Pozzatti, and Bonnie Massimino, MEd. Without this team of outstanding colleagues and authors, all devoted to excellence in helping children and their families thrive, this series would not be possible.

I am grateful to all of the families that have trusted me to care for and support them throughout my years in clinical practice. Thank you for working collaboratively with me on the mission to create more meaningful and healthier lives for you and yours.

Thank you to my mentors, past and present, who helped me build instrumental skills, believed in my goals, and fostered my passion to help others by guiding me with compassion, patience, and grace: Dr. Bonnie Zucker, Dr. Erika Martinez, Dr. Melanie V. Hsu, Dr. Lydia V. Flasher, Ann Lyke, MEd, Dr. Emily Shumate, Dr. Lourdes Suarez-Morales, Dr. Diana Formoso, Dr. Rebecca Bulotsky Shearer, Dr. Jill Ehrenreich-May, Dr. Amy L. Beaumont, Dr.

Dulce Jané, Dr. Yukari Tomozawa, and Dr. Jason Baker.

Thank you to my best friend and forever golden girl, Alana Greer, whose compassion, commitment to authenticity, and support is a lighthouse I can always count on. As you know, my love for you transcends space and time. Para mi Palomita, I can't wait to meet you, love you, and help you navigate all the beautiful things this world has to offer. Titi Silvi loves you always.

Finally, I'd like to thank my family. My mom, Silvia, dad, Bernardo, and brother, Bernie, who have been patient with me as I've dedicated my life to helping others and work towards my ever-expanding dreams. Your unconditional love and support mean the world to me.

BIBLIOGRAPHY

CHAPTER 1

Baloran, E. T. (2020). Knowledge, attitudes, anxiety, and coping strategies of students during COVID-19 pandemic. *Journal of Loss and Trauma, 25*(8), 1–8. https://doi.org/10.1080/15325024.2020.17 69300

Centers for Disease Control and Prevention. (2018, December 20). *Data and statistics on children's mental health.* https://www.cdc. gov/childrensmentalhealth/data.html

Ghandour, R. M., Sherman, L. J., Vladutiu, C. J., Ali, M. M., Lynch, S. E., Bitsko, R. H., & Blumberg, S. J. (2019). Prevalence and treatment of depression, anxiety, and conduct problems in US children. *The Journal of Pediatrics, 206*, 256-267.e3. https://doi. org/10.1016/j.jpeds.2018.09.021

Gosch, E. A., Flannery-Schroeder, E., Mauro, C. F., & Compton, S. N. (2006). Principles of cognitive-behavioral therapy for anxiety disorders in children. *Journal of Cognitive Psychotherapy, 20* (3), 247–262. https://doi.org/10.1891/jcop.20.3.247

Grills-Taquechel, A. E., Norton, P., & Ollendick, T. H. (2010). A longitudinal examination of factors predicting anxiety during the transition to middle school. *Anxiety, Stress & Coping, 23*(5), 493–513. https://doi.org/10.1080/10615800903494127

Hofmann, S. G., Asnaani, A., Vonk, I. J. J., Sawyer, A. T., & Fang, A. (2012). The efficacy of cognitive behavioral therapy: A review of meta-analyses. *Cognitive Therapy and Research, 36*(5), 427–440. https://doi.org/10.1007/s10608-012-9476-1

Irawan, A. W., Dwisona, D., & Lestari, M. (2020). Psychological impacts of students on online learning during the pandemic COVID-19. *KONSELI : Jurnal Bimbingan Dan Konseling (E-Journal), 7*(1), 53–60. https://doi.org/10.24042/kons.v7i1.6389

Ishikawa, S. (2015). A cognitive-behavioral model of anxiety disorders in children and adolescents. *Japanese Psychological Research, 57*(3), 180–193. https://doi.org/10.1111/jpr.12078

Jones, C. (2020, May 13). *Student anxiety, depression increasing during school closures, survey finds.* EdSource. https://edsource.org/2020/student-anxiety-depression-increasing-during-school-closures-survey-finds/631224

Kendall, P. C., & Southam-Gerow, M. A. (1996). Long-term follow-up of a cognitive–behavioral therapy for anxiety-disordered youth. *Journal of Consulting and Clinical Psychology, 64*(4), 724–730. https://doi.org/10.1037/0022-006x.64.4.724

Mazzone, L., Ducci, F., Scoto, M. C., Passaniti, E., Genitori D'Arrigo, V., & Vitiello, B. (2007). The role of anxiety symptoms in school performance in a community sample of children and adolescents. *BMC Public Health, 7*(347) https://doi.org/https://doi.org/10.1186/1471-2458-7-347

Seligman, L. D., & Ollendick, T. H. (2011). Cognitive-behavioral therapy for anxiety disorders in youth. *Child and Adolescent*

Psychiatric Clinics of North America, 20(2), 217–238. https://doi.
org/10.1016/j.chc.2011.01.003

CHAPTER 2

Alavi, N., & Omrani, M. (2018a). Understanding and rating our
feelings, and the thought record. *Online Cognitive Behavioral
Therapy*, 69–79. https://doi.org/10.1007/978-3-319-99151-1_7

Alavi, N., & Omrani, M. (2018b). What are automatic thoughts?
Online Cognitive Behavioral Therapy, 81–91.
https://doi.org/10.1007/978-3-319-99151-1_8

Deak, J. M., & Ackerley, S. (2017). *Your fantastic elastic brain: Stretch
it, shape it*. Little Pickle Press.

CHAPTER 3

American Academy of Sleep Medicine. (2012). *Healthy sleep habits
and good sleep hygiene*. http://sleepeducation.org/essentials-in-
sleep/healthy-sleep-habits

Berkheiser, K. (2018, June 14). *9 Health Benefits of Vitamin B12,
Based on Science*. Healthline. https://www.healthline.com/
nutrition/vitamin-b12-benefits

Centers for Disease Control and Prevention. (2021, February 15).
Childhood Nutrition Facts. https://www.cdc.gov/healthyschools/
nutrition/facts.htm

Centers for Disease Control and Prevention. (2020, April 21).
Physical Activity Facts. https://www.cdc.gov/healthyschools/
physicalactivity/facts.htm#:~:text=Regular%20physical%20
activity%20can%20help

Donoghue, C., & Meltzer, L. J. (2018). Sleep it off: Bullying and sleep disturbances in adolescents. *Journal of Adolescence, 68*, 87–93. https://doi.org/10.1016/j.adolescence.2018.07.012

Gulia, K. K., & Kumar, V. M. (2020). Importance of sleep for health and wellbeing amidst COVID-19 pandemic. *Sleep and Vigilance.* https://doi.org/10.1007/s41782-020-00087-4

Learning ZoneXpress. (2011). *MyPlate lesson plan.* Retrieved June 1, 2021, from https://www.uen.org/cte/facs_cabinet/downloads/FoodNutritionI/S2O2MyPlateLessonPlans.pdf

Mayo Clinic. (2018). *How much exercise do your kids need?* https://www.mayoclinic.org/healthy-lifestyle/fitness/expert-answers/kids-and-exercise/faq-20058336

Nemours KidsHealth. (2022). *MyPlate food guide.* https://kidshealth.org/en/kids/pyramid.html

Options For Youth. (2016, August 25). *The importance of eating healthy for students.* https://ofy.org/blog/the-importance-of-eating-healthy-for-students/

Schuster, K., Learning, Center, D., & Institute, D. of C. T. at the C. M. (2021). *Encouraging good sleep habits.* Child Mind Institute. https://childmind.org/article/encouraging-good-sleep-habits/

Stanford Medicine Children's Health. (n.d.). *Exercise and teenagers.* https://www.stanfordchildrens.org/en/topic/default?id=exercise-and-teenagers-90-P01602

Suni, E. (2020, August 14). *What is sleep hygiene?* Sleep Foundation. https://www.sleepfoundation.org/sleep-hygiene

The Nutrition Source. (2017a, March 21). *Kid's healthy eating plate.* https://www.hsph.harvard.edu/nutritionsource/kids-healthy-eating-plate/

US Department of Health and Human Services. (2015) *2015-2020 Dietary Guidelines—health.gov.* Health.gov. https://health.gov/dietaryguidelines/2015/guidelines/

Wheaton, A. G., Jones, S. E., Cooper, A. C., & Croft, J. B. (2018). Short sleep duration among middle school and high school students — United States, 2015. MMWR. *Morbidity and Mortality Weekly Report, 67*(3), 85–90. https://doi.org/10.15585/mmwr.mm6703a1

Xie, X., Dong, Y., & Wang, J. (2018). Sleep quality as a mediator of problematic smartphone use and clinical health symptoms. *Journal of Behavioral Addictions, 7*(2), 466–472. https://doi.org/10.1556/2006.7.2018.40

CHAPTER 4

Battistin, J. M. & Owen, C. (2019). *Mindfulness for teens in 10 minutes a day : Exercises to feel calm, stay focused & be your best self.* Rockridge Press.

Bazzano, A. N., Anderson, C. E., Hylton, C., & Gustat, J. (2018). Effect of mindfulness and yoga on quality of life for elementary school students and teachers: results of a randomized controlled school-based study. *Psychology Research and Behavior Management, Volume 11,* 81–89. https://doi.org/10.2147/prbm.s157503

Bluth, K., & Eisenlohr-Moul, T. A. (2017). Response to a mindful self-compassion intervention in teens: A within-person association of mindfulness, self-compassion, and emotional well-being outcomes. *Journal of Adolescence, 57,* 108-118.

Caballero, C., Scherer, E., West, M. R., Mrazek, M. D., Gabrieli, C. F. O., & Gabrieli, J. D. E. (2019). Greater mindfulness is associated with better academic achievement in middle school. *Mind, Brain, and Education, 13*(3), 157–166. https://doi.org/10.1111/mbe.12200

Gates, M., & Libvanderploeg. (2018). *This moment is your life (and so is this one) : A fun and easy guide to mindfulness, meditation, and yoga.* Dial Books.

Garcia Sanchez, A. (2022, May 7). *Home.* WholeHearted School Counseling. https://wholeheartedschoolcounseling.com/

Halloran, J. (2020). *Coping skills for teens workbook : 60 helpful ways to deal with stress, anxiety and anger.* Coping Skills For Kids/ Encourage Play Llc.

Martinez, T., & Zhao, Y. (2018). The impact of mindfulness training on middle grades students' office discipline referrals. *RMLE Online, 41*(3), 1–8. https://doi.org/10.1080/19404476.2018.1435840

Mindful (2017, January 11). *Jon Kabat-Zinn: Defining mindfulness.* https://www.mindful.org/jon-kabat-zinn-defining-mindfulness/

Mindful. (2020, July 8). *What is mindfulness?* https://www.mindful.org/what-is-mindfulness/

CHAPTER 5–7

Bagus Hernowo, T. (2021). The effectiveness of cognitive behavior therapy (CBT) to reducing anxiety of 6th grade elementary school students who will face the national exam. *International Journal of Research Publications, 80*(1). https://doi.org/10.47119/ijrp100801720212066

Berman, J. (2021). *Self-regulation workbook for kids: CBT exercises and coping strategies to help children handle... anxiety, stress, and other strong emotions.* Ulysses Pr.

Burns, D. D. (2017). *Feeling Good : The New Mood Therapy.* Blackstone Audio, Incorporated.

Calero, A. D., Barreyro, J. P., & Injoque-Ricle, I. (2018). Emotional intelligence and self-perception in adolescents. *Europe's Journal of Psychology, 14*(3), 632–643. https://doi.org/10.5964/ejop.v14i3.1506

Clark, D. A., & Beck, A. T. (2012). *The anxiety and worry workbook : The cognitive behavioral solution.* Guilford Press.

Comer, J. S., Hong, N., Poznanski, B., Silva, K., & Wilson, M. (2019). Evidence base update on the treatment of early childhood anxiety and related problems. *Journal of Clinical Child & Adolescent Psychology, 48*(1), 1–15. https://doi.org/10.1080/15374416.2018.1534208

Ehrenreich-May, J., & Pinto, S. S. (2018b). *Unified protocol for transdiagnostic treatment of emotional disorders in children : Workbook.* Oxford University Press.

Goff, S. (2021). *Brave: A teen girl's guide to beating worry and anxiety.* Bethany House.

Greenberger, D., & Padesky, C. A. (2015). *Mind over mood : Change how you feel by changing the way you think.* The Guilford Press.

Kendall, P. C., & Hedtke, K. A. (2006). *The coping cat workbook.* Workbook Publishing.

Kodal, A., Fjermestad, K., Bjelland, I., Gjestad, R., Öst, L.-G., Bjaastad, J. F., Haugland, B. S. M., Havik, O. E., Heiervang, E., & Wergeland, G. J. (2018). Long-term effectiveness of cognitive behavioral therapy for youth with anxiety disorders. *Journal of Anxiety Disorders, 53*(53), 58–67. https://doi.org/10.1016/j.janxdis.2017.11.003

MacCann, C., Jiang, Y., Brown, L. E. R., Double, K. S., Bucich, M., & Minbashian, A. (2020). Emotional intelligence predicts academic performance: A meta-analysis. *Psychological Bulletin, 146*(2), 150–186. https://doi.org/10.1037/bul0000219

Sánchez-Álvarez, N., Berrios Martos, M. P., & Extremera, N. (2020). A meta-analysis of the relationship between emotional intelligence and academic performance in secondary education: A multi-stream comparison. *Frontiers in Psychology, 11*. https://doi.org/10.3389/fpsyg.2020.01517

Sigurvinsdóttir, A. L., Jensínudóttir, K. B., Baldvinsdóttir, K. D., Smárason, O., & Skarphedinsson, G. (2019). Effectiveness of cognitive behavioral therapy (CBT) for child and adolescent anxiety disorders across different CBT modalities and comparisons: A systematic review and meta-analysis. *Nordic Journal of Psychiatry, 74*(3), 1–13. https://doi.org/10.1080/0803948 8.2019.1686653

Usán Supervía, P., Salavera Bordás, C., & Murillo Lorente, V. (2020). Psychological analysis among goal orientation, emotional intelligence and academic burnout in middle school students. *International Journal of Environmental Research and Public Health, 17*(21), 8160. https://doi.org/10.3390/ijerph17218160

Whiteside, S. P. H., Sim, L. A., Morrow, A. S., Farah, W. H., Hilliker, D. R., Murad, M. H., & Wang, Z. (2019). A meta-analysis to guide the enhancement of CBT for childhood anxiety: Exposure over anxiety management. *Clinical Child and Family Psychology Review, 23*(1), 102–121. https://doi.org/10.1007/s10567-019-00303-2

Zucker, B. (2016). *Anxiety-free kids : An interactive guide for parents and children*. Routledge.

CHAPTER 8

Achor, S. (2018). *The happiness advantage : How a positive brain fuels success in work and life*. Currency.

Cohn, M. A., Fredrickson, B. L., Brown, S. L., Mikels, J. A., & Conway, A. M. (2009). Happiness unpacked: Positive emotions increase life satisfaction by building resilience. Emotion, 9(3), 361–368. https://doi.org/10.1037/a0015952

Dixson, D. D. (2020). How hope measures up: Hope predicts school variables beyond growth mindset and school belonging. Current Psychology. https://doi.org/10.1007/s12144-020-00975-y

Hurley, K. (2020). *A year of positive thinking for teens : Daily motivation to beat stress, inspire happiness, and achieve your goals.* Rockridge Press.

In, H. (2022). Longitudinal and reciprocal relationships between self-esteem, school adjustment, and happiness in Korean secondary school students. *School Psychology International,* 014303432110724. https://doi.org/10.1177/01430343211072426

Kyoung Hwang, Y., & Lee, C. S. (2018b). Relationship between stress and happiness in middle school students: Dual mediation effect of growth mindset and self-esteem. *Medico-Legal Update,* 18(1), 248. https://doi.org/10.5958/0974-1283.2018.00053.1

Lyubomirsky, S. (2008). *The how of happiness : A practical guide to getting the life you want.* Penguin Books.

Napawan, A. (2021). *Happiness workbook: A CBT-based guide to foster positivity and embrace joy.* Rockridge Press.

Seligman, M. E. P. (2002). *Authentic happiness : Using the new positive psychology to realize your potential for lasting fulfilment.* Nicholas Brealey Publishing.

Seligman, M. E. P. (2018). *Optimistic child.* Nicholas Brealey Publishing.

CHAPTER 9

Bernstein, J. (2019). *The stress survival guide for teens : CBT skills to worry less, develop grit, & live your best life.* Instant Help Books, An Imprint Of Harbinger Publications, Inc.

Bounce Back Project. (n.d.). *Resilience is made up of five pillars: Self awareness, mindfulness, self care, positive relationships & purpose.* https://www.bouncebackproject.org/resilience/

Brougham, L., & Kashubeck-West, S. (2017). Impact of a growth mindset intervention on academic performance of students at two urban high schools. *Professional School Counseling, 21*(1), 2156759X1876493. https://doi.org/10.1177/2156759x18764934

Dumont, M. & Provost, M.A. (1999). Resilience in adolescents: Protective role of social support, coping strategies, self-esteem, and social activities on experience of stress and depression. *Journal of Youth and Adolescence 28*, 343–363.

Duckworth, A. (2016). *Grit: The power of passion and perseverance.* New York Scribner.

Dweck, C. (2016). *What having a "growth mindset" actually means.* https://leadlocal.global/wp-content/uploads/2016/12/Dweck-What-Having-a-%e2%80%9cGrowth-Mindset%e2%80%9d-Actually-Means-HBR.pdf

Dweck, C. S. (2006). *Mindset: The new psychology of success.* Random House.

Kyoung Hwang, Y., & Lee, C. S. (2018). Relationship between stress and happiness in middle school students: Dual mediation effect of growth mindset and self-esteem. *Medico-Legal Update, 18*(1), 248. https://doi.org/10.5958/0974-1283.2018.00053.1

Li, Y., & Bates, T. C. (2020). Testing the association of growth mindset and grades across a challenging transition: Is growth mindset associated with grades? *Intelligence, 81*, 101471. https://doi.org/10.1016/j.intell.2020.101471

Shrivastava, A., & Desousa, A. (2016). Resilience: A psychobiological construct for psychiatric disorders. *Indian journal of psychiatry, 58*(1), 38–43.

Zeng, G., Hou, H., & Peng, K. (2016). Effect of growth mindset on school engagement and psychological well-being of chinese primary and middle school students: The mediating role of resilience. *Frontiers in Psychology, 7*. https://doi.org/10.3389/fpsyg.2016.01873

CHAPTER 10

Feeney, D. M. (2021). Positive self-talk: An emerging learning strategy for students with learning disabilities. *Intervention in school and clinic,* 105345122110148. https://doi.org/10.1177/10534512211014881

Helmstetter, S. (2017). *What to say when you talk to yourself: Powerful new techniques to program your potential for success!* Gallery Books.

Kim, J., Kwon, J. H., Kim, J., Kim, E. J., Kim, H. E., Kyeong, S., & Kim, J.-J. (2021). The effects of positive or negative self-talk on the alteration of brain functional connectivity by performing cognitive tasks. *Scientific Reports, 11*(1), 14873. https://doi.org/10.1038/s41598-021-94328-9

Shadinger, D., Katsion, J., Myllykangas, S., & Case, D. (2019). The impact of a positive, self-talk statement on public speaking anxiety. *College Teaching,* 1–7. https://doi.org/10.1080/87567555.2019.1680522

Tuhovsky, I. (2017). *The science of self talk*. Createspace Independent Publishing Platform.

Walter, N., Nikoleizig, L., & Alfermann, D. (2019). Effects of Self-Talk Training on Competitive Anxiety, Self-Efficacy, Volitional Skills, and Performance: An Intervention Study with Junior Sub-Elite Athletes. *Sports, 7*(6), 148. https://doi.org/10.3390/sports7060148

Zucker, B. (2016). *Anxiety-free kids: An interactive guide for parents and children*. Routledge.

ABOUT THE AUTHOR

Silvi Guerra, PsyD, is a licensed psychologist specializing in the treatment of anxiety disorders and related conditions. She practices at Bonnie Zucker & Associates, a group private practice in Rockville, Maryland. Known to her clients as "Dr. Silvi," her treatment approach incorporates an evidence-based, empathic, culturally-informed, and resilient methodology to psychotherapy with clients and their families. Dr. Silvi is also fluent in Spanish and provides (bilingual) culturally-sensitive therapeutic services to clients from multicultural backgrounds. Dr. Silvi completed her postdoctoral fellowship at Johns Hopkins School of Medicine and Kennedy Krieger Institute's Behavior Management Clinic. She completed her pre-doctoral training at Lucile Packard Children's Hospital at Stanford University and the Community Clinic at Children's Health Council (CHC). Dr. Silvi received her doctoral degree from Nova Southeastern University and her bachelor's degree in psychology from the University of Miami.

Visit bonniezuckerandassociates.com

ABOUT THE ILLUSTRATOR

DEANDRA HODGE is an illustrator and designer based in Washington, DC. She received her Bachelor of Arts in Fine Arts, concentrating in Graphic Design, from University of Montevallo.

Visit @deandrahodge_ on Instagram.

KID CONFIDENT

1

KID CONFIDENT #1

HOW TO MANAGE YOUR
SOCIAL POWER
IN MIDDLE SCHOOL

by Bonnie Zucker, PsyD • illustrated by DeAndra Hodge

"Guide for fostering a happy adolescence by maneuvering its challenges and pitfalls...The lively design, including playful illustrations, makes for accessible reading, with ideas unpacked into digestible pieces."—Kirkus

2

KID CONFIDENT #2

HOW TO MASTER
YOUR MOOD
IN MIDDLE SCHOOL

by Lenka Glassman, PsyD • illustrated by DeAndra Hodge

"An excellent mental health resource for adolescents and those who support them...illustrations and diagrams support the text, making subjects... more accessible...Packed with valuable material, this volume is an informative read for middle schoolers who struggle with their emotions." —Kirkus

3

KID CONFIDENT #3

HOW TO HANDLE
STRESS
FOR MIDDLE SCHOOL SUCCESS

by Silvi Guerra, PsyD • illustrated by DeAndra Hodge

"This well-organized and practical guide to stress management is a great choice for upper elementary and middle school libraries."—Kirkus

4

KID CONFIDENT #4

HOW TO
NAVIGATE
MIDDLE SCHOOL

by Anne Pezzetti, PhD, & Bonnie Massimino, MEd • illustrated by DeAndra Hodge